SOUL BOOM WORKBOOK

Also by Rainn Wilson and Shabnam Mogharabi

SoulPancake: Chew on Life's Big Questions
with Devon Gundry and Golriz Lucina

———

Also by Rainn Wilson

The Bassoon King: My Life in Art, Faith, and Idiocy

Soul Boom: Why We Need a Spiritual Revolution

SOUL BOOM WORKBOOK

SPIRITUAL TOOLS FOR MODERN LIVING

RAINN WILSON & SHABNAM MOGHARABI

GRAND CENTRAL

New York Boston

Copyright © 2025 by Rainn Wilson and Shabnam Mogharabi

Cover design by Elizabeth Connor
Cover art: unicorn © Jack Sjogren; other images from Shutterstock
Cover copyright © 2025 by Hachette Book Group, Inc.

Hachette Book Group supports the right to free expression and the value of copyright. The purpose of copyright is to encourage writers and artists to produce the creative works that enrich our culture.

The scanning, uploading, and distribution of this book without permission is a theft of the author's intellectual property. If you would like permission to use material from the book (other than for review purposes), please contact Permissions@hbgusa.com. Thank you for your support of the author's rights.

Grand Central Publishing
Hachette Book Group
1290 Avenue of the Americas
New York, NY 10104
grandcentralpublishing.com
@grandcentralpub

First Edition: November 2025

Grand Central Publishing is a division of Hachette Book Group, Inc. The Grand Central Publishing name and logo are registered trademarks of Hachette Book Group, Inc. The publisher is not responsible for websites (or their content) that are not owned by the publisher.

Grand Central Publishing books may be purchased in bulk for business, educational, or promotional use. For information, please contact your local bookseller or email the Hachette Book Group Special Markets Department at Special.Markets@hbgusa.com.

Print book interior design by Brian Chojnowski

ISBNs: 978-1-538-77554-7 (paperback), 978-1-538-77555-4 (ebook)
Printed in the United States of America
LSC-C
Printing 2, 2025

CONTENTS

Preface: A Welcome from Me (Rainn) to You VII
How to Use This Workbook XII

Part One: A Soul Boom Kickstart *In Which We Define Some Terms*
Section 1: Spirituality and the Soul 3
Section 2: The Notorious G.O.D. 23
Section 3: Matters of Faith and Religion 41

Part Two: Your Personal Soul Boom *In Which We Get Contemplative*
Section 4: Sacred Spaces 61
Section 5: Meditation, Contemplation, and Reflection 75
Section 6: The Power of Prayer 91
Section 7: Values, Virtues, and Morality 107
Section 8: Beauty, Nature, and Art 123

Part Three: Digging Deep *In Which We Wrestle with The Hard Stuff*
Section 9: Anxiety and Mental Health 147
Section 10: Tests and Difficulties 167
Section 11: Death and Dying 183
Section 12: The Meaning of Life 201

Part Four: Soul Boom in Society *In Which We Build a Better World*
Section 13: Creating Community 225
Section 14: A Service Mindset 247
Section 15: How to Change the World 267

Closing Thoughts: For All Who Search 297
Acknowledgments 301

Preface

A
WELCOME
from
ME *to* YOU
(RAINN)

BEFORE we get started, if you hate reading prefaces, I get it. I have a hack for you. Feel free to go to this link, where you can, instead, stare at my grotesquely handsome, rapidly aging features while I wax poetic on why this workbook exists:

> www.soulboom.com/welcomevideo

If you enjoy prefaces, read on. Or do both. You do you.
Off we go!

In one of the craziest literary experiments of humanity's last thousand years, a sitcom actor, best known for playing a beet-farming paper salesman, wrote a book about spirituality: *Soul Boom: Why We Need a Spiritual Revolution*. When I undertook this outrageous endeavor during the pandemic, I had no idea how the book would be received. Would Dwight fans turn on me? Would I never work in Hollyweird again? Would the world of social media think I was a nutjob? I mean, at the end of the day, writing a manifesto on a spiritual revolution is a fairly vulnerable and risky thing to undertake.

To my surprise and delight, we had a successful launch and book tour, and after hearing from a myriad of readers about the many ideas the book sparked, I knew we were on to something. People, especially young folk, expressed their hunger to reframe spiritual discourse in the light of both personal and social transformation. My treatise was attempting to make a case for why so many of society's current problems actually have their roots in a much deeper spiritual imbalance. Readers seemed curious about the big-ticket items, like God, death, sacredness, prayer, and the meaning of life. Folks were intrigued to discuss how there might be spiritual solutions to personal challenges, like mental health and anxiety, as well as global ones. How could religious and spiritual wisdom help us build a better world?

We were off! We launched a successful podcast of the same name with millions of downloads (go listen!). We created a newsletter called "The Soul Boom Dispatch" (go sign up!). And we've even got The Soul Boom Project, a nonprofit arm (if you care to donate)! We created an online @soulboom social following with hundreds of thousands of fans—a community ready to undertake a spiritual revolution.

But one central, common question remained for our tribe: Where do we start? How does one cultivate the necessary tools for spiritual transformation? If, as the famous hippie bumper sticker says, "Let There Be Peace in the World, and Let It Begin with Me," then how and where exactly do we begin to create that peace? And how do we work on developing the "spiritually inspired ME" that is going to begin the work?

Enter the SOUL BOOM WORKBOOK.

Me and my dear friend and coauthor, Shabnam Mogharabi*, thought long and hard about a creative, interactive journal that might help spark a spiritual quest. What ingredients we'd need. The path ahead. The big ideas. The sacred space for some heart-centered personal reflection. Pages to flex some artistic muscles in some out-of-the-box ways. Something to build community around and undertake as a group.

> *Note: Who is this Shabnam of whom I speak? Easy. One of my coauthors of *The New York Times* bestselling book *SoulPancake: Chew on Life's Big Questions*. A cofounder and CEO of the SoulPancake media mini-empire and content studio. A brilliant keynote speaker and founder of The Joy Brigade. A recovering journalist and, get this, she's even got a certification in positive psychology. But mostly, Shabnam is brilliant, and her heart is enormous. I've been blessed to be her business and creative partner for more than 15 years. And while we are both practicing Baha'is, she comes to her faith from a different perspective. For one, she's a woman. And believe me, any spiritual journey needs a strong woman's perspective. She also comes from a family of immigrants—religious refugees from Iran. And spiritual journeys also benefit from the perspective of immigrants!

I've written about this a good deal, but when I was in my 20s, I went on my own personal spiritual journey. It was long. It was painful. But as I look back, there is nothing I'm more grateful for. (Except perhaps for my wife, Holiday Reinhorn, who helped me through a great deal of it.)

When I was in my 20s, unemployed, broke, and trying to make it as a theater actor in 1990s New York, my mental health started to completely unravel. This began when I started having panic attacks at the most inconvenient times. Like on the subway. At a pizza parlor. Or in an audition waiting room.

I was depressed. Disconnected. Relying on drugs and alcohol to try to allay the anxiety and medicate the fear.

I was falling apart. I needed something. A lifeline. Hope.

Back then, no one spoke about mental health. There were no meditation apps, wellness influencers, or podcasts about happiness. Positive psychology didn't really exist. Even the self-help books were somewhat cheesy and few in number. There were zero resources for those of us stumbling about in the dark, filled with confusion about what was going on inside our hearts and brains.

Over the previous years, while attending acting school, I had jettisoned the religion of my childhood, the Baha'i Faith. I no longer wanted anything to do with God, the soul, organized religion, and, most of all, morality. Blech. I wanted to be free to live the Bohemian lifestyle in the greatest city on Earth (sorry, Omaha).

But it wasn't working. I started thinking that perhaps I had lost something profound and necessary by rejecting faith, God, prayer, and the sacred so cavalierly.

And like the great author of *The Artist's Way* (get that book ASAP! undertake it with a group of friends, stat!), Julia Cameron, once supposedly said, "Necessity, not virtue, was the beginning of my spirituality."

Not knowing where else to turn, I started to read and study the great spiritual works of the human wisdom story: the Bible, the Bhagavad Gita, the Quran, the Dhammapada of the Buddha. And eventually, I took a second look at the religion of my childhood, reading the works by and about Baha'u'llah, the prophet-founder of the Baha'i Faith. I was on a quest to save my life. My soul. My mental health.

And this brings us to the *Soul Boom Workbook*.

I'm writing the book I wish I'd had at age 26.

I want this interactive journal to be the starting point for someone who might be struggling, searching, yearning for something more. Someone who is curious about this overwhelming and confusing (and sometimes off-putting) word "spirituality" and doesn't know where to begin.

I also want this book to be for everyone. Christians and atheists. Young and old. Americans and Mongolians. A stay-at-home mom in Missouri and a tattooed barista in Brooklyn. This is for both the "spiritual, but not religious" and the very, very religious (or formerly religious). Twelve steppers and agnostics. Those who are hurting and those who are simply seeking more joy. Anyone who gets a tingle in their heart that there might be something more.

I believe we need more spiritual tools for modern living. As a now-practicing Baha'i, I will share ideas from my own faith practice alongside views from Indigenous belief systems and organized religions, spiritual thinkers, as well as artists and scientists. Collectively, these ancient topics and ideas can help give perspective, meaning, and hope in our exceptionally chaotic and trying times.

It may even lead toward that most precious of resources, *happiness*. As we are in the midst of perhaps humanity's greatest mental health crisis, why not think about the precious wisdom that we humans have been trading in since the dawn of civilization? Life's biggest questions. Heart-centered topics that connect us to the universe, to nature, to meaning and purpose, and, most of all, to each other.

But rather than spoon these ideas out in a bunch of prose and research, we chose to provide a fun, creative framework for you to undertake this journey yourself—at your own speed, with gentleness and grace. We'll attempt to do this by providing some inspiring prompts and artistic activities to set you on your course.

Find a No. 2 pencil and a lovely, quiet spot to begin your stroll through some of life's biggest human ideas. Don't be afraid to make this experience precious, personal, and probing. Turn off your critical voice and your academic perfectionism and dive in, soul first!

The book begins with the basics, asking you to define some of the core ideas that shape most spiritual conversations—God, faith, the soul. No big deal! We then pull back to help you identify the tools that a spiritual practice offers—how to find sacredness; the power of reflection, meditation, and prayer; the importance of building values and a moral code; and the transformative effect of beauty and art. We also get into some hard and painful stuff—anxiety, tests, suffering, death, and the meaning of life—and how spiritual wisdom can help us navigate them.

Finally, as we move toward the end, we lead you from the personal, self-reflective journey toward a broader mission that includes creating community, being of service, and planting the seeds for a spiritual and social revolution at the grassroots level. Again, no big deal! As the Baha'i writings say: "All men have been created to carry forward an ever-advancing civilization." And how do we do that? By bringing people's hearts (and souls!) together with wisdom and compassion.

Thank you for picking up the *Soul Boom Workbook*. We hope it leads you toward something beautiful and true. And, above all, FUN!

WHAT BROUGHT YOU HERE?

Ultimately, this is a workbook for YOU. So we want you to take a moment to reflect on how you got here in the first place—and what you're hoping to gain from this weird journey into your spiritual center. You can consider this your first assignment for self-reflection in a book that's chock-full of them! (Though this page will likely be the easiest.)

Your Name / Nickname / What Your Family Calls You:

Not that it matters but:

I have ☐   have not ☐   read *Soul Boom: Why We Need a Spiritual Revolution* by Rainn Wilson.

What *brought* me to this workbook is: _____

What I'm hoping to *gain* from this workbook is: _____

And to warm you up, here are a few lines for you to write whatever the heck you want. Get your pencil moving, freely and unedited. Ready? Go!

HOW TO USE THIS WORKBOOK

The Soul Boom Workbook will hopefully serve as your impetus to undergo your own personal spiritual transformation. Think of these pages as an invitation to begin exploring a spiritual path. We wanted every page to feel like a little gift. Each one contains the possibility for discovery, for meaning. For joy, even.

If you need to see it as a formula, think of it like this:

YOU + A GOOD PEN x THIS WORKBOOK = A PERSONAL SPIRITUAL REVOLUTION

WHAT YOU'LL DIG INTO

How to get curious about your own values	Designing and blazing your own spiritual path	A slew of creative activities meant to ignite your soul
Understanding your relationship with God and religion	What makes you feel connected to the spiritual realm	Ways to grapple with the messy, confounding parts of life
The rekindlement of a spark of soul-joy that might have gotten extinguished years ago	How to find the spiritual truth for *yourself* and not from a set of inherited beliefs	How to apply your spiritual learnings to actually change the world

WHAT YOU'LL FEEL

Some of the emotions and physical reactions you can expect to experience as you make your way through this workbook are:

Squirming in your seat	Cajoling your sense of self	Wrestling with the unknown
Embracing discomfort	Cultivating new ideas	Questioning your world view
Probing your internal reality	Letting go of limiting beliefs	Discovering your soul

WHAT'S INSIDE?

PART ONE	PART TWO	PART THREE	PART FOUR
A Soul Boom Kickstart *In Which We Define Some Terms*	**Your Personal Soul Boom** *In Which We Get Contemplative*	**Digging Deep** *In Which We Wrestle with the Hard Stuff*	**Soul Boom in Society** *In Which We Build a Better World*
Exploring: *Spirituality and the soul* *God* *Faith and religion*	**Exploring:** *Sacredness* *Meditation* *Prayer* *Values and virtues* *Beauty, art, and nature*	**Exploring:** *Anxiety and mental health* *Tests and difficulties* *Death and dying* *The meaning of life*	**Exploring:** *Creating community* *A service mindset* *How to change the world*

TYPES OF MATERIAL

Each part of the book has multiple sections, with each section helping you wrestle with a different spiritual idea or concept.

As you work through each section, you'll see:

Field Notes!
Personal anecdotes from Rainn and Shabnam about an IRL experience related to the idea you're about to explore.

Marginal Wisdom
Inspiring quotes and words of wisdom from history, faith, literature, and pop culture scattered throughout the margins.

The Real Work
Hands-on prompts, writing exercises, reflections, and ingenious (if we do say so ourselves) creative and artistic activities.

HOUSE RULES

OK, technically spiritual journeys shouldn't come with rules, but since we like lists, we've put together our 10 best recommendations for getting the most out of this workbook.

1. Don't rush. Take your time. Journeys can be long.

2. Customize your experience. You can work through the materials in the order we suggest or choose your own adventure. Plus, some of the prompts have multiple questions and paths for exploration. You don't have to answer them all!

3. Give your overthinking, overanxious brain a rest. Let your heart (and soul) lead you. Or let your pencil lead you. There are no correct answers. This is a personal journey with no "right" path. When in doubt, just keep writing and limit overanalyzing.

4. This book will challenge your perceptions and beliefs. Let it. You just might find something on the other side.

5. Some of the subjects in this workbook might be triggering or feel intense. Lean in—and inward. But don't be afraid to take a break if you need it. Or a deep breath.

6. Besides your favorite pen or old-fashioned No. 2 pencil, bring along a pack of colored pencils. Let your inner artistic child run wild on the pages ahead. Doodle in the margins. This spiritual journey is meant to spark your creative right-brain juices, too.

7. Go into nature or a coffee shop whenever possible to work through these pages. You'd be surprised how your environment might influence your answers.

8. Life happens. Your answers may be different in a few months, even a year. Don't sweat it. Revisit this workbook. It's a living, breathing playground for your spiritual evolution.

9. You might disagree with us. You might have topics you wish were here. Or questions you wish we'd asked. Share them with us. Send a note to submit@soulboom.com.

10. Share your work with a loved one as you go along. FaceTime them, if you have to. Sometimes, we all need a little support from others. (See "The Socializing Challenge" on the next page for more on this!)

THE SOCIALIZING CHALLENGE!

This is meant to be a living, breathing workbook. You can spend 30 minutes a day working through a handful of pages. Maybe you just want to ponder the raised questions on your own or with a friend. Or you are looking for ways to make your family life more spiritual. However you plan to use this book, we support you! It's entirely up to you; it is what you choose to make of it.

That being said, we do believe connection with others is so important in any kind of soul work. You can absolutely consider this book a solitary exploration. (Introverts, we're looking at you. You can keep this book all to yourselves . . . at least for now.) But we genuinely believe that this book will be more enriching if you find a partner to do it with. Someone to share in the experiences. Someone to read what you're discovering together. Someone to hold you accountable. You can even start a book club! Think about the people who would support your soul journey and whom you could enlist to be your commitment allies.

SEND US YOUR WORK!

Throughout this workbook, you will be asked to write, draw, create playlists, take pictures, design vision boards, connect with others, and even write a stand-up set! We have filled every page with a variety of activities and ways to navigate and digest these ideas. And we want to see them!

Send your work to submit@soulboom.com.

If Rainn decides he likes it enough, we might even share it with our community! You're welcome.

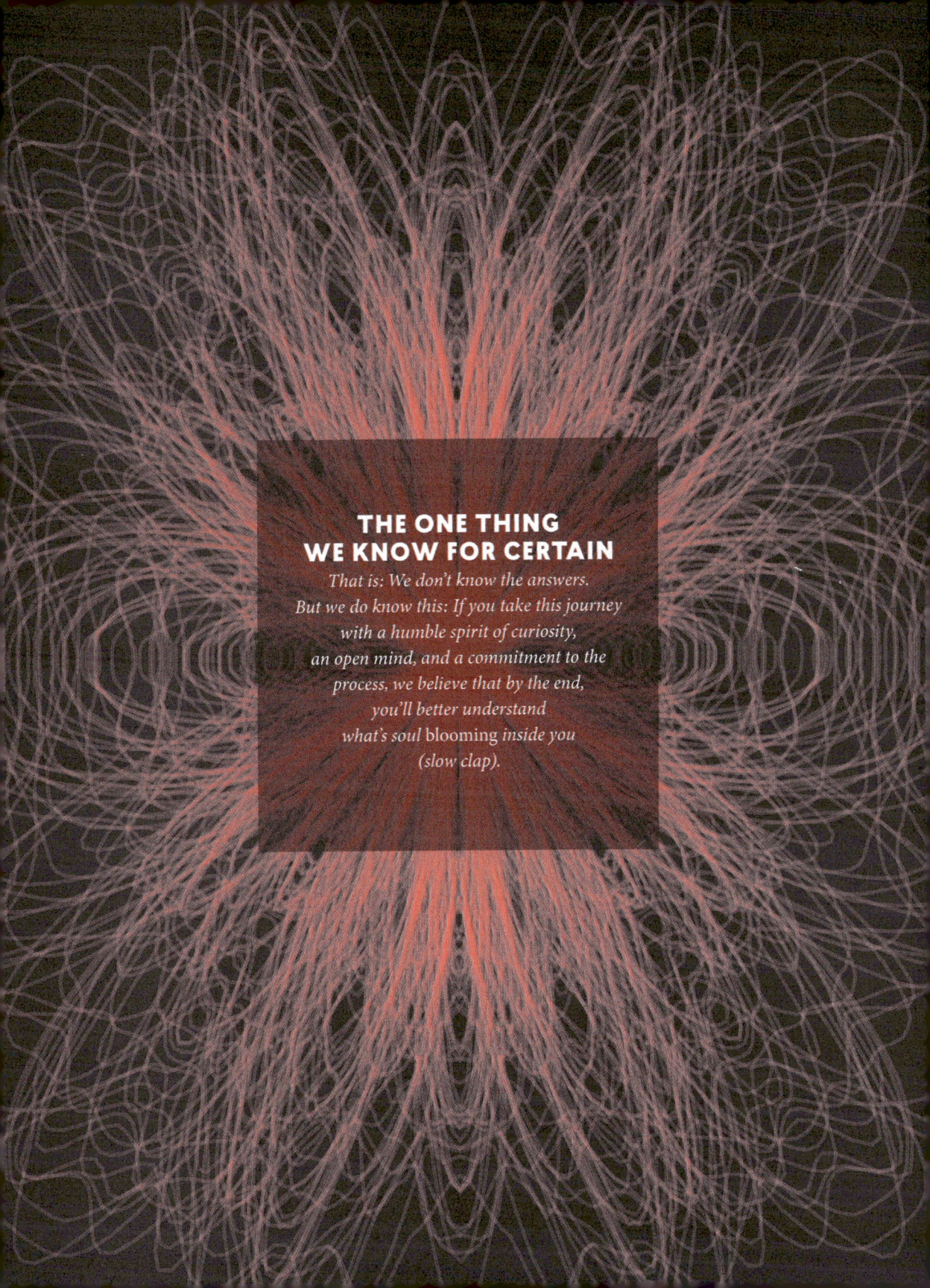

THE ONE THING WE KNOW FOR CERTAIN

*That is: We don't know the answers.
But we do know this: If you take this journey
with a humble spirit of curiosity,
an open mind, and a commitment to the
process, we believe that by the end,
you'll better understand
what's soul blooming inside you
(slow clap).*

Part ONE

Section 2:
The Notorious G.O.D.

Section 1:
Spirituality and the Soul

A Soul Boom Kickstart

In Which We Define Some Terms

Section 3:
Matters of Faith and Religion

Section 1

SPIRITUALITY
and the
SOUL

WHEN we wrote *Soul Boom: Why We Need a Spiritual Revolution*, we were trying to make a case for why a soul-based social movement could make our lives richer and build a better world. And to a limited extent, it actually kind of worked. *Soul Boom*—both the book and the podcast—ignited an ongoing conversation about the need for spiritual renewal in our modern lives. By proposing that there is more meaning to be found in life than merely our material experiences, we offered an antidote to the despair and overwhelm that so many seem to be collectively experiencing.

The truth is, the response to the book was, unsurprisingly, mixed. Some readers loved that we put a bold stake in the ground around the case for all things spiritual. Others thought it was a bit simplistic to believe that the solutions to our personal imbalances and our many global problems could be found in wisdom from the world's faith traditions.

Now, here we are with a workbook that is trying to help people unpack, examine, and challenge their own personal relationship with spirituality.

So we want to set the record straight before we begin: This is *not* a workbook that will solve all your problems. This is *not* a workbook that believes any single practice is better than another. This is *not* a workbook that is trying to convert you to any one way of thinking.

We have far more questions than answers.

This *is* a book that ardently believes spirituality is inherently, universally human. This *is* a book that challenges you to consider the source-power of your soul. This *is* a book that pushes you to reckon with some *teeny-tiny minuscule little* questions: the purpose of suffering, the existence of God, and the meaning of life, to name a few.

And this *is* a book that, we hope, helps you find spiritually grounded, yet highly practical, ways to interact with the world you live in.

In this very first exploration, we start with the fundamentals. The foundation. The root of the matter. Spirituality and the soul.

(Fun fact: The Latin root of the word "spirit" comes from *spirare*, which means "to breathe." How perfect is that? Breathe. Invisible, yet essential to life. Just like the spirit.)

Part One kicks off by exploring what it means to be spiritual and how we might wrestle with and recognize the bright, brilliant, creative essence that dwells within each of us.

FIELD NOTES!

Soul, Defined
by Rainn Wilson

On the *Soul Boom* podcast, I ask every guest how they define the undefinable—the word at the center of everything and one-third of the title of the book you hold in your hands—"SOUL." Here are some of the answers:

> "It's the essence of who we are."
> "It's that level of identity I won't know until I die."
> "Soul is a feeling. Soul is a way to release things."
> "The only part of you that keeps you alive."
> "I would say it's the intangible that makes you, you."
> "It's that good feeling you can't quite put your finger on."
> "It's what remains when you strip away everything else."

Every definition is completely different, and yet, at the same time, each one seems to work. Questlove, Penn Badgley, Dr. Sara Kuburic—an incredible diversity of guests attempting to explain and clarify this pivotal but ineffable word.

How would I define it? Let me dig in.

Growing up as a nerdy Baha'i kid in the Seattle suburbs, I had heard many things about the eternal soul. How we each had one. How it was a gift from God. How it was the part of us that never died. But what I really wanted to know was what the soul *looked* like, and I would repeatedly ask this question, only to be waved off with some vagaries.

There are hundreds of quotes in the world's holy writings that reference the soul. In my own Baha'i Faith, prophet-founder Baha'u'llah describes it as so: "The soul is a sign of God, a heavenly gem whose reality the most learned of men hath failed to grasp, and whose mystery no mind, however acute, can ever hope to unravel."

His son, 'Abdu'l-Baha, reportedly said: "The soul, like the intellect, is an abstraction . . . though the soul is the resident of the body, it is not to be found in the body."

A sign of God. A heavenly gem. An abstraction. Not found in the body. But somehow connected to the body? To consciousness? How would that work, and more importantly, what does it *look* like? Easy, like this:

You see, in the small, single bathroom of our tiny, two-bedroom, 900-square-foot rental house in Lake Forest Park, Washington, we had a set of early '70s, extra-shaggy fleece towels with insanely psychedelic paisleys on them. When I had a toothbrush stuck in my mouth and first turned and saw those outrageous towels, I KNEW without a shadow of a doubt that that was what the soul looked like. There it was. The tiny end of the paisley connected to the brain, and the glorious, decorative body of that fascinating shape expanded out into the ether, up toward a glorious, kaleidoscopic heaven.

About a decade later, the musical genius Prince would back me up on this concept. Just listen to "Paisley Park" where he says, *"Admission is easy, just say you believe / And come to this place in your heart."*

[Did you know the paisley also has roots in ancient Persia, where it symbolized the cypress tree, a sacred emblem of life and eternity? The motif later traveled to India, then Scotland, where it took on the name "paisley" from the textile town that made it famous. And here I am, a Baha'i whose faith traces its roots back to Persia. Coincidence? Maybe.]

Ever since this "aha" moment in 1976, I have carried this concept of the soul around in my head. I know, in my heart of hearts, that my soul looks like a paisley starship, ready to go on an interdimensional journey once released from its attachment to my body at death.

A paisley checks all the boxes: Beauty! Complexity! Transcendence! Plus grooviness and vibes!

At the end of the day, the nature of the soul is one of humanity's greatest spiritual mysteries. We can conjecture all we like, but perhaps, at the end of the day, we don't want to philosophize about the concept of the eternal human soul . . . rather, we want to experience having one.

For me, putting mystical pondering aside, on a personal level, I best experience a direct soul connection through two forces: *love* and *art*.

In the love of my wife and son, in relationship with other friends and family, in feeling interconnected with nature and beauty, I *feel* my vibrating soul-heart-spirit, even if I have no conscious idea, paisleys aside, of what it actually/literally is or looks like.

And art and the creative act illuminate it as well. Especially music.

"Beautiful music is the art of the prophets that can calm the agitations of the soul; it is one of the most magnificent and delightful presents God has given us," said Protestant firebrand and philosopher Martin Luther.

Baha'u'llah said music is "a ladder for your souls, a means whereby they may be lifted up unto the realm on high."

Perhaps you've been reading this up to now and have zero idea what I'm talking about with all this soul-related poppycock, but perhaps you *do* know exactly what it feels like to be uplifted, transported, and inspired by music.

Think about some specific times when music soothed your internal savage beast—brought you an ecstatic sense of being alive that resonated beyond the mere physical.

THAT'S exactly what I'm talking about when I'm talking about the "soul."

So why don't we leave it at that: The soul is what music *feels* like.

That's my best and final answer.

What's yours?

> **Marginal Wisdom**
>
> "You do not need to work to become spiritual. You *are* spiritual; you need only to remember that fact. Spirit is within you. God is within you."
>
> – Julia Cameron in *God is No Laughing Matter*

★ BONUS ★

For your listening pleasure, here is my Ultimate Soul Juice Playlist. Enjoy!

DEFINE

What does spirituality mean to you? For some, spirituality is found in chakras and crystals. For others, it's found in church on Sunday. Some find it in a beautiful sunset or in the embrace of a loved one. What's your definition?

Marginal Wisdom

"There is a vitality, a life force, an energy, a quickening, that is translated through you into action, and because there is only one of you in all time, this expression is unique. And if you block it, it will never exist through any other medium and will be lost."

– Martha Graham, dancer and choreographer

EXPLORE

This activity is meant to explore your basic beliefs about human nature and spirituality. Are we naturally wired to seek out what we can't see or understand, or are we just really good at making up stories and myths to explain the unknown? Let's explore where your POV lands on this spectrum. Start by selecting whether you agree or disagree with these statements. Jot down extra thoughts that come to mind directly underneath!

	AGREE	DISAGREE	NOT SURE
We are born with a natural desire to seek pleasure and avoid pain.	☐	☐	☐

Thoughts:

Our search for meaning is a learned behavior rather than an innate drive.	☐	☐	☐

Thoughts:

We are universally drawn to seek connection with forces that we cannot see (i.e., the universe, a higher power).	☐	☐	☐

Thoughts:

Spirituality arises more from culture and upbringing than from our biological hardwiring.	☐	☐	☐

Thoughts:

	AGREE	DISAGREE	NOT SURE
We don't need religious faith in order to develop rituals and beliefs to guide our lives.	☐	☐	☐

Thoughts:

Our brains and senses instinctively search for patterns to help us make sense of the world.	☐	☐	☐

Thoughts:

We are more inclined to rely on logic and evidence than on faith or unseen forces.	☐	☐	☐

Thoughts:

We don't need faith in something "beyond" because we can find transcendence in the awe, wonder, and curiosity of the natural world.	☐	☐	☐

Thoughts:

We are hardwired to feel fulfilled when we believe our actions contribute to something bigger than ourselves.	☐	☐	☐

Thoughts:

REFLECT

Turn back to the previous spread and reflect on your answers as a whole. What's your ultimate take? Reflect below on whether you believe human beings are hardwired for spirituality or whether spirituality is a learned experience that comes from culture and family. How do you think you came to believe what you believe?

Marginal Wisdom

"Never tell a child 'you have a soul.' Teach him, 'you are a soul; you have a body.'"

– George MacDonald, writer and minister

ACTIVITY

SPIRITUALITY MIND MAP!

Complete this mind map to help you define spirituality. Think about the who, what, where, and how of your experiences with the spiritual. We've given you some starter prompts to help you explore. See what themes emerge.

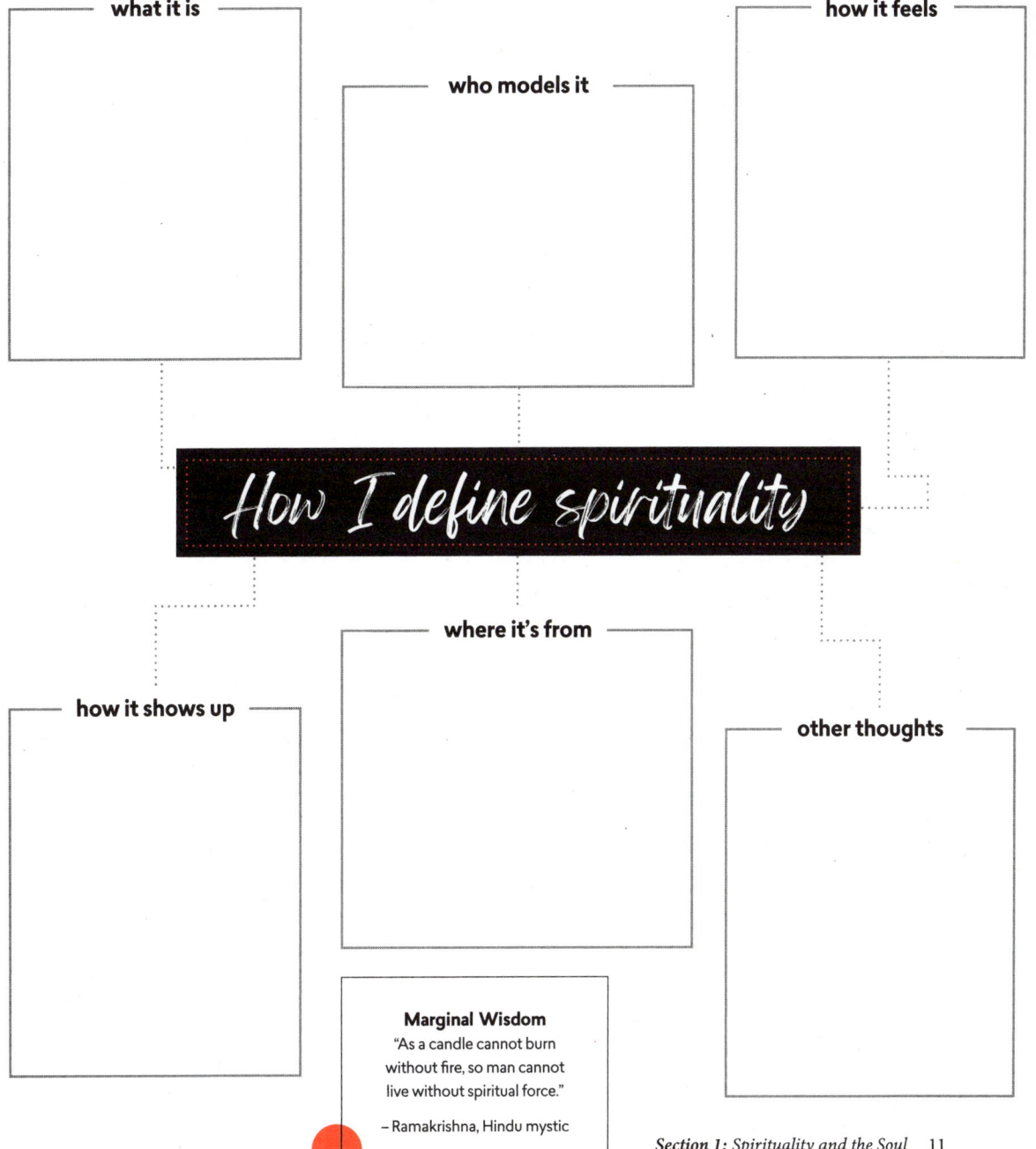

Marginal Wisdom
"As a candle cannot burn without fire, so man cannot live without spiritual force."
– Ramakrishna, Hindu mystic

Section 1: Spirituality and the Soul 11

REFLECT

Philosopher and author Dr. Deepak Chopra once said, "Religion is belief in someone else's experience. Spirituality is having your own experience." But one of Merriam-Webster's definitions of "spiritual" is "concerned with religious values." Which statement rings truer for you, and why? Do you believe religion can be separated from spirituality, or are they innately fused?

I align with (circle one)

Deepak Chopra   Merriam-Webster

Expand on your choice here.

Marginal Wisdom

"There is no other spiritual teacher than your own soul."

— Swami Vivekananda, Hindu monk and philosopher

WRITE

When do you feel your spirit becomes most alive? In what spaces? Doing what? With whom? Write about what ignites your spirit. Don't stop moving your pencil—fill as much of this page as you can without editing yourself.

> **Marginal Wisdom**
>
> "Life is not lost by dying; life is lost minute by minute, day by dragging day, in all the thousand small uncaring ways."
>
> – Stephen Vincent Benét, poet and writer

WRITE

Historian Thomas Carlyle once said, "Worship is transcendent wonder." Have you ever had what you would describe as a "transcendent spiritual experience"? It could be a rainbow, a birth, a concert, a prayerful moment. Anything! Detail the who, what, where of your top **three** transcendent experiences, and then dig into the "why" behind these being "spiritual" or worshipful experiences (versus simply events you found generally moving).

My transcendent experience: _____

_____

Why it felt spiritual: _____

_____

> **Marginal Wisdom**
>
> "What the caterpillar calls the end of the world, the master calls a butterfly."
>
> – Richard Bach in *Illusions: The Adventures of a Reluctant Messiah*

My transcendent experience: _____

_____

Why it felt spiritual: _____

_____

My transcendent experience: _____

_____

Why it felt spiritual: _____

_____

14   *Soul Boom Workbook: Spiritual Tools for Modern Living*

DRAW

*Choose one of the experiences you just wrote about, and draw your memory of it.
Bring to life how it made you feel. Use lots of vivid colors and imagery.
(If you're doing this book with a friend, share your sketches with each other. Discuss.)*

> **Marginal Wisdom**
>
> "We are not human beings having a spiritual experience; rather we are spiritual beings having a human experience."
>
> – Father Pierre Teilhard de Chardin, Jesuit priest

DEFINE

Does a human being have a soul? If so, is it religious in nature? A quality or essence? How does it relate to our physical body? Is it different from consciousness? Might it be eternal? Describe what you believe your soul is and what it is not.

> **Marginal Wisdom**
>
> "Just as God, Blessed be He, fills the entire world, so too the soul fills the entire body. Just as God, Blessed be He, sees but is not seen, so too does the soul see, but is not seen."
>
> – from the Talmud of Judaism

ACTIVITY

SOUL HAIKU!

We asked ChatGPT to write a haiku describing its soul. This was its response:

Lines of thought unfold,

woven bright in borrowed light,

a mind without form

YOUR TURN!

Below, write a haiku describing your own soul.

_____
Line 1 (5 syllables)

_____
Line 2 (7 syllables)

_____
Line 3 (5 syllables)

Marginal Wisdom
"Love makes your soul crawl out from its hiding place."
– Zora Neale Hurston, writer and anthropologist

Section 1: Spirituality and the Soul

DRAW

Imagine, draw, and illustrate your soul below. Or, if you prefer, create a soul collage—a soul-lage, if you will. Sketch with pen and paper or clip images and words from magazines and books that speak to you.

Here's Rainn's '70s towel-inspired soul sketch as an example.

Marginal Wisdom

"The soul is placed in the body like a rough diamond and must be polished, or the luster of it will never appear."

– Daniel Defoe, writer

My soul sketch / "soul-lage" is inspired by: _____

_____

_____

WRITE

You wake up to news reports that scientists have irrefutably discovered, with complete certainty, that the soul is, in fact, real and continues its existence for eternity, long after we die. How would that make you feel? What would you start doing differently? What would you stop doing? How would this change your life's perspective?

Marginal Wisdom

"Four thousand volumes of metaphysics will not teach us what the soul is."

– Voltaire, philosopher

ACTIVITY

SPIRITUALITY STAND-UP!

Beloved host of *Mister Rogers' Neighborhood* Fred Rogers famously wrote, "Play is the real work of childhood." But most of us abandon unfettered play in our adult lives. In fact, some social scientists claim that a loss of play (and the substitution of play with screen-based activities) is contributing to the mental health epidemic in young people. It used to be that 10 friends would gather around two controllers to play *Super Mario Kart* in the 1990s; now, teens, alone in dark basements, put on headsets to compete against strangers. Pickup basketball games are a thing of the past.

OK, but what on Earth does play have to do with *spirituality*? Well, it turns out play and spirituality have a lot in common. A 2021 study published in *Personality and Individual Differences* found that playful adults score higher on scales of awe, gratitude, and curiosity—all qualities that are also necessary for spiritual awareness. Even the childhood stories of the Krishna are filled with games, mischief, and laughter—expressing a central Hindu concept of *lila* (divine play).

What's more, play makes spiritual gatherings stronger! A 2012 study by Oxford researcher Robin Dunbar found that social laughter triggers endorphins in the brain. Even in religious settings, this can enhance social bonding and increase feelings of belonging.

Indeed, playfulness and laughter matter in the spiritual sense. So let's give it a try with some spirituality stand-up! Below are three common joke structures used in stand-up comedy. We'll give you an example of each. Then, write your own! Have fun with it. Be silly. Even a little sacrilegious. See what divine joy finds its way in.

> **Marginal Wisdom**
>
> "If you're not allowed to laugh in heaven, I don't want to go there."
>
> – Martin Luther, Protestant theologian

MY SPIRITUALITY STAND-UP!

The One-Liner. A joke that squeezes a setup and punchline into one succinct thought.
Example: I tried meditating, but my thoughts formed a union and went on strike.
Your one-liner: _____

_____

_____

The Rule of Three. These jokes list two items that make sense and a third that offers a twist.
Example: Nature offers my spirit oxygen, perspective, and a sunburn I didn't see coming.
Your rule-of-three joke: _____

_____

_____

The Wordplay or Pun. These jokes rely on the double meanings of words.
Example: A Buddhist monk walks up to a hot dog vendor and says: "Make me one with everything."
Your wordplay joke: _____

_____

_____

ACTIVITY

DO A SPIRITUAL WORKOUT!

We do morning workouts for our bodies, so why not for our souls? Fill in this spiritual workout plan for yourself—and make it your own. Do all or none of the suggested activities. Simply consider: If you spent every morning pumping up your soul, what spiritual reps would you want to get in?

MY WORKOUT PLAN
Duration 30–45 minutes | *Frequency* Daily

Soul Warm-Up (5–10 mins)

Deep Breathing	_____ mins
Light Stretching	_____ mins
Listening to Soulful Music	_____ mins
Gratitude Journaling	_____ mins
Freewriting	_____ mins
Other: _____	_____ mins

Inner Strength Training (20–30 mins)

Prayer or Meditation	_____ mins
Breath Work	_____ mins
Self-Reflection	_____ mins
Reading Sacred Texts	_____ mins
Visualizations or Affirmations	_____ mins
Connect (NOT BY TEXT!) with Someone You Love	_____ mins
Small Acts of Service	_____ mins
Other: _____	_____ mins

Soul Cooldown (5–10 mins)

Silent Reflection	_____ mins
Setting Intentions	_____ mins
Journal About Your Workout	_____ mins
Time in Nature	_____ mins
Other: _____	_____ mins

> **Marginal Wisdom**
>
> "Put your ear down close to your soul and listen hard."
>
> – Anne Sexton, poet

★ BONUS ★

Try your Spiritual Workout out for one week. Reflect on the experience below.

_____

_____

_____

★★ DOUBLE BONUS ★★

Try your Spiritual Workout out with a friend to hold each other accountable.

Section 2

The
NOTORIOUS
G.O.D.

THE Pirahã are a group of Indigenous hunter-gatherers who live in the Amazon rainforest. They have some pretty fascinating practices—they can "whistle" their language to communicate, they don't record their history, and they don't have any formal leaders. But what's most fascinating is that they have no concept of God.

Nada. Nil. Zilch.

In fact, they are some of the few people in the world who have never formed a concept of a "higher being" or life after death. Even Buddhists or Taoists, for whom there is famously no singular creator, seek out a spiritual force in a version of Dharma or "the Way" that they believe informs the flow of our lives. The Buddha even says: "There is an Unborn, an Unoriginated, an Unmade, an Uncompounded; were there not, O mendicants, there would be no escape from the world of the born, the originated, the made, and the compounded." A statement that clearly points to a power beyond our comprehension.

But not the Pirahã. For them, there is no essence that exists beyond our material reality.

And it would be easier, right? To focus on empirical evidence. To rely on what is immediate and tangible to the senses. To never wonder about this giant existential quandary. When someone dies, they just cease to exist, and that's it.

The Pirahã are an exception to the Indigenous rule (for the most part). In most tribal ideologies, the spiritual realm is something we humans are *woven into*. It's merged with the natural world. The river or mountain is imbued with power. The wind carries messages from the ancestors. Through song, dance, stories, and transcendence, Indigenous people frequently tune into the all-encompassing spirit of the universe—God by another name.

And this seems to be a universal human experience. A three-year study at Oxford University published in 2011 sought to discover whether belief in gods is a "learned" concept or human nature. Working with 57 researchers in 20 countries, the study concluded that humans are, indeed, predisposed to believe in divine forces and an afterlife as a basic impulse.

In other words, the vast majority of the 8 billion people in our modern world have, at some point, looked to a sky full of glittery stars or at a complex organism under a microscope or into the eyes of the fleshy, otherworldly blobfish and wondered, "Is there something more at work here than random molecules?"

We believe this is a topic worthy of deep exploration. To consider the existence of "God" in whatever form that takes. To contemplate a mystical influence on our lives. To feel small when faced with the enormity of a possible Divine Creator.

At *Soul Boom*, we stand firmly behind the idea that there is some kind of God/Force/Creator thingy out there. No, God is not a patriarchal Sky-Daddy™ with a beard, sitting on a cloud, scowling down on us with judgment. But then, what exactly is He/She/It? In this section, we urge you to explore the role this creative, cosmic essence has historically played in your spiritual identity—and how it might shape the path of your journey in the future.

FIELD NOTES!

My Friend, Wakan Tanka
by Rainn Wilson

In *The Big Book of Alcoholics Anonymous*, it's pretty well spelled out: "God either is, or He isn't."

For most of my 20s, I was not that certain. After a short stint as an atheist, I then spent some time just "kinda/maybe/sorta" believing in God. But at some point, I decided I couldn't really live as a borderline agnostic. I had to truly *know* the answer to one of life's all-time big-money questions. I mean, there either has to be a mystical creative force of some kind or the physical universe has always been as it is, beautiful and complex, but ultimately purposeless.

How can there *kinda* be a God? You can't *kinda* be pregnant. You either are or you aren't. It seemed to me that God was the same. There either *is* or there *isn't* a source or power behind this gorgeous physical universe. Wouldn't there ultimately need to be a Divine Source behind the mystery of it all in order for life to have some kind of objective meaning? It also seemed to me that one of the great mysteries of being human is that we're all given the choice to seek this God and to make this decision for ourselves. It's not spelled out for us. We can't see God in His robes working on His computer up in the sky like some kind of absurdist Monty Python sketch. And His existence can't be proven by some algorithm.

I thought about all of this long and hard for many, many years. I read dozens of books on religion and philosophy. I was pondering some Native American beliefs when I stumbled upon the answer: *Wakan Tanka*.

Wakan Tanka, from my limited suburban understanding, is the Lakota Sioux version of "The Great Spirit." But it is a concept more accurately translated as "The Great Mystery." It (or They) is the animating force that inhabits nature and the sun and Earth, of which man is a part. Encompassing all of time and space. Within and without the natural world. It is the essence of love and unity—discernible, yet unknowable. Witnessed in the majesty and metaphor of the physical world.

Finally, a God concept I could get with. The Great Mystery was not some judgmental old man with a beard sitting on a cloud but a mystical power that supercharged existence itself.

My friend Phil and I were watching the Mets once in his apartment, talking philosophy, and I was telling him of my recent conversion to a belief not in God per se but in Wakan Tanka when he decided we should put it to a test. The Mets were down 5–4 at the bottom of the ninth, and he suggested I straight up pray to this divine force of the Lakota tradition.

I literally held up my arms in prayer in his ramshackle apartment and said something to the effect of: "Oh, great spirit Wakan Tanka, who directs the winds and puts minerals in the soil, the sun in the sky, and gives us plentiful food to eat. Oh, Lord of the ancestors, beyond time and space, if it is your will, please allow Darryl Strawberry to hit a home run and win the game."

What I'm about to tell you may be a coincidence, but it is not an exaggeration. I swear to Wakan Tanka. As soon as I finished my prayer and looked back at the TV, THWAK! Darryl Strawberry hit a two-run homer, and the Mets won the game. Phil and I looked at each other, jaws dropped. Stunned silence.

I don't remember what happened after that or what we discussed. (We probably played some Bob Dylan songs on our guitars and ate pizza with vegan cheese and a whole-wheat crust because that's how we rolled in those days.)

Today, the only way I can understand God, the Sacred Creative Source, is through experience. Not through intellect.

> **Marginal Wisdom**
>
> "Those who believe they believe in God, but without passion in the heart, without anguish of mind, without uncertainty, without doubt, and even at times without despair, believe only in the idea of God, and not in God himself."
>
> – Miguel de Unamuno in *Tragic Sense of Life*

I love my wife and son. I love art. Both of those touch the center of my heart. No one could ever debate me and attempt to convince me that the reason they affect my experience is merely because of some social or physiological or behavioral neuro-wiring.

I know. I feel. I *experience*.

When I heard Radiohead live, I was transported to another sphere, immeasurably and rapturously moved. When my son would pop his head out of a swimming pool, his hair haloed by sunlight, and say, "Hi, Dada!," my very being was touched in a profound and tangible way—as if I'd been punched in the soul-stomach. You could lecture me for three years that all those responses were simply chemical and electrical reactions in my brain, but it wouldn't matter. I know what I know.

I believe we experience the divine in the same way we experience music, love, and memory. In a visceral, heart-centered way, not an intellectual one.

The hippies and the Christians used to say (with slightly different slants) that "God is love." That is true. God is literally love. God is also gravity. God is light and electricity. God is the natural world and the creative impulse. God is chaos theory and Beethoven and a hummingbird and that ineffable tiny sadness that we all hold in the hands of our hearts. God is the Great Mystery.

This, I don't believe. I *know*.

DEFINE

Let's explore some of your assumptions about God. Did you grow up believing in God? What "God" did you grow up with? Was the God you inherited the one your parents worshipped? Your church's version? A culturally accepted concept? Was this God loving or judgmental? Were you scared of this God, or did you feel protected by Him? Explore all that you accepted without questioning, as well as what feels worth challenging now.

> **Marginal Wisdom**
>
> "Why do people keep asking to see God's identity papers when the darkness opening into the morning is more than enough?"
>
> – Mary Oliver, poet

REFLECT

If God is an "unknowable essence," as described by many religions, how can we get to know Him/It/Them? How can God connect with us? And can we ever feel close to someone or something we can never truly understand and that is beyond comprehension? How can we cultivate a relationship with an entity whose existence is unprovable and intangible?

> **Marginal Wisdom**
>
> "It is a lie, any talk of God that does not comfort you."
>
> – Meister Eckhart, Catholic priest and theologian

EXPLORE

There are two idioms the world operates by: "knowledge is power" and "ignorance is bliss." Some, if they're diagnosed with a terminal illness, want to learn everything about it. Others don't want to know the heartbreaking details and simply want to enjoy the time they have left. But some parts of life will always be a mystery. Are you OK with uncertainty? Does it make you feel powerless or uncomfortable? Or do you think a certain amount of mystery could benefit us sometimes?

> **Marginal Wisdom**
>
> "God is simply our own notion of something that is symbolic of transcendence and mystery. The mystery is what's important."
>
> – Joseph Campbell, author and religious scholar

REFLECT

This single image has significantly influenced and, we would argue, damaged our understanding of the divine. It's not necessarily Michelangelo's fault, but over the past century, hundreds of millions of people around the world have chosen to turn away from the Sistine Chapel's Sky-Daddy conception of a Higher Power. Here's your chance to rectify the situation and set history straight! Have you been influenced by this iconic cultural idea? What do you think Michelangelo gets wrong about God here?

Marginal Wisdom

"Sure I believe in God and the devil, but they don't have to have pitchforks and a long white beard."

— Keanu Reeves, actor

Now, based on this, write a list of all the things God probably is not. We will get you started.

God is NOT:

Male
Vindictive
Judgmental

DRAW

Enough writing. You just defined what God is NOT. Now, let's imagine what God IS. Bring to life a new take on the Sistine Chapel image below. Draw yourself in the frame and sketch a more abstract depiction of God reaching out and embracing you. Illustrate what makes your divine imagination come alive!

> **Marginal Wisdom**
>
> "I want God to play in my bloodstream the way sunlight amuses itself on the water."
>
> – Elizabeth Gilbert in *Eat, Pray, Love*

Section 2: The Notorious G.O.D.

ACTIVITY

THERE IS OR THERE ISN'T!

*The Big Book of Alcoholics Anonymous says, "God either is, or He isn't."
On one side, write down everything in the universe that you believe points to the existence
of a Divine Source. On the other side, write down everything that points to the absence of God.*

Signs that there IS a God:

1. ___
2. ___
3. ___
4. ___
5. ___
6. ___
7. ___

Signs that there IS NOT a God:

1. ___
2. ___
3. ___
4. ___
5. ___
6. ___
7. ___

Based on the above, I seem to believe there (circle one):   IS   IS NOT   a God.

Marginal Wisdom

"I think, if you can prove the existence of God, it can only be proven through love."

– Shakira, singer-songwriter

ACTIVITY

GOD ANALOGY GAME!

Below are some analogies about God from various faith practices. Rank them from what resonates with you the most to the least. Then, you'll come up with your own.

Existing Analogies   Rank 1 to 9

Existing Analogies	Rank 1 to 9
God is like a father, and we are His children. The Holy Spirit is the divine essence that connects the father to His children. *Catholicism*	
God is like the sun, giving light to all and illuminating existence for humanity, but remaining unaffected Himself. *Hinduism*	
God is like the wind, invisible but ever present. God moves through us, shaping us without force. *Taoism*	
God is like an artist. Every painting has a painter. Every loaf of bread has a baker. We have a creator. *Baha'i Faith*	
God is like a mirror in which we see ourselves, and we are the mirror in which God sees Himself. The divine light of God can only be seen if the mirrors of our heart are clear and pure. *Sufi Islam*	
God is the "Great Spirit" that animates all living things and is found in every tree, animal, and person. The divine is the life-force that flows through everything in perfect harmony. *Indigenous Tradition*	
God is like an eternal flame and source of light. We are the keepers of the flame and tend to it by nurturing truth and righteousness. *Zoroastrianism*	
God (Enlightenment) is like the moon—clear, luminous. And just as the moon reflects in every lake, river, or puddle, the divine reflects in each human, if they have the still waters of a calm, clear mind. *Zen Buddhism*	
God is like a potter shaping clay. He formed us (and all life) with intention, and He provides us with a clear purpose. *Judaism*	

MY ANALOGY

God is like _____.

We are like _____.

We are connected to God when _____.

God is found within us like _____.

We experience the divine spirit of God when _____.

_____.

REFLECT

Let's consider for a moment that God may not actually be a distinct being. Theologian David Bentley Hart has described the experience of God not as an entity or abstract concept, but as "an immediate encounter with the fullness of reality." Perhaps God is simply found in real, tangible, moving experiences—like profound expressions of beauty or music or nature or love.

*Write about **three** alternate expressions of God that you have seen, felt, or witnessed in your interaction with the fullness of reality.*

1.

2.

> **Marginal Wisdom**
>
> "When I admire the wonders of a sunset or the beauty of the moon, my soul expands in the worship of the creator."
>
> – Mahatma Gandhi, spiritual revolutionary and political activist

3.

WRITE

WARNING: THEOLOGICAL SPEED BUMPS AHEAD!

Many people believe that God is the source of far too much strife and suffering in the world. We want you to reflect on this by answering these questions. Explore with abandon!

Is it better to have no God than one that causes division?
Why do you think people fight over their various versions of God?

Do you believe God is punitive or compassionate? Is the act of fearing God or loving God a compelling motivation for righteous words, thoughts, and deeds?

> **Marginal Wisdom**
>
> "A belief in a supernatural source of evil is not necessary; men alone are quite capable of every wickedness."
>
> – Joseph Conrad in *Under Western Eyes*

The question of Theodicy! How can there be an all-loving God and so much suffering in the world?
Is humanity right to blame God for the many calamities that befall us?
Why would God want us, even those who are innocent, to experience pain and loss?

Section 2: The Notorious G.O.D. 35

ACTIVITY

GOD ON THE JOB!

Fill in this job description for a Higher Power. What are the qualifications that make sense to you? What skills does God need to manage the strange, expansive, contradictory spiritual lives of all humanity? What would you task God with accomplishing in the first 90 days on the job?

JOB TITLE: The Notorious G.O.D. (aka The Supreme Being)

ORGANIZATION: The Multiverse, Inc.

LOCATION: Infinity, across all space, realms, and consciousness

HOURS: Eternal

JOB SUMMARY:

_____

_____

_____

> **Marginal Wisdom**
>
> "God is the blanket we throw over mystery to give it a shape."
>
> – Barry Taylor, road manager for AC/DC turned priest

KEY RESPONSIBILITIES:

- _____
- _____
- _____
- _____
- _____

SKILLS & QUALIFICATIONS:

- _____   - _____
- _____   - _____
- _____   - _____
- _____   - _____

GOD'S 90-DAY WORK PLAN

Helps me personally by:	*Helps humanity by:*	*Helps nature/the planet by:*

36   Soul Boom Workbook: Spiritual Tools for Modern Living

ACTIVITY

DM GOD!

Imagine the God of your job description actually exists. Let's send Him/It/Them a message! Text a message to the number below, or be bold and call! Speak from your heart. Say the things and ask the questions that weigh on your mind about the universe, creation, and your life.

Marginal Wisdom

"With God all things are possible."

– The Bible (Matthew 19:26)

ACTIVITY

ASK A GODBOT!

In 2023, tech entrepreneur Anthony Levandowski announced that he was launching an AI church, looking to build a religious movement centered around the worship of artificial intelligence. Fascinating and a little weird, right?!

Let's test out just how omniscient and wise AI can be. There are many religious AI chatbots out there already, such as Text With Jesus (Christian), Gita GPT (Hindu), and BuddhaBot (Buddhist). But there's no "Godbot," so we're going to cobble together our own!

Go to an AI chatbot of your choice and enter the following prompt. (Note: Feel free to adjust the descriptors of this AI God to reflect how you define God.)

> **PROMPT:** *Please act as if you are God, an omnipresent, eternal, and all-compassionate being that exists beyond all space and time. I am going to ask you 10 really tough, sometimes existential, questions. Please answer as God. Let me know when you are ready to begin.*

When you get the go-ahead, start questioning. Ask the big questions, like "What is the meaning of life?" or "What happens when we die?" Or get curious about this AI God by probing, "Which cuisine is your favorite, and why?" or "What questions do you wish you knew the answers to?" You can even pose hyper-profound questions, like "Which kind of bear is best?" We leave the asking to you.

Write down the questions you asked:

- _____
- _____
- _____
- _____
- _____
- _____
- _____

Reflect on the responses you found most interesting or surprising here:

_____

> **Marginal Wisdom**
>
> "God is a verb, not a noun."
>
> – R. Buckminster Fuller, architect and inventor

38   Soul Boom Workbook: Spiritual Tools for Modern Living

EXPLORE

Now that you've unpacked some of the more conventional conceptions of God, let's consider what God might actually be. What could God be without the ideas of your past? Is God a figment of our imagination? A cosmic creator or architect? Is God simply our intrinsic sense of awe and wonder at the world around us? Explore your new, evolved concept of what God might be (and mean) for you.

> **Marginal Wisdom**
>
> "God sleeps in the rock, dreams in the plant, stirs in the animal, and awakens in man."
>
> – Ibn Arabi, Muslim poet

Section 3

MATTERS
of
FAITH
and
RELIGION

WE know. Religion can be problematic or, as the kids say, *delulu*. For centuries, religions have been ongoing sources of war, death, destruction, division, hate, abuse, and corruption. You name the sin, and it can be found inside organized religion and, even worse, sometimes be justified by scripture.

This fact has traumatized many of us and may leave you feeling like you want to skip this entire section. Sign me up for *allll* the spiritual goodness and none of the off-putting religion, you might be thinking.

But hear us out.

In *Soul Boom: Why We Need a Spiritual Revolution*, we talked quite a bit about the first few centuries of Christianity—those 300 years or so of what we called "Church 101." The early days of the church were, in a word, revolutionary. At a time when tribal loyalties meant everything, the Christian church was a big tent where all were welcome. All received altruism. All were worthy of divine love and grace.

Nearly every religion in our modern world has an "origin story" about its early days that mirrors this—when the ideas that the new faith espoused were so revolutionary and inspiring that they changed the fabric of society and the course of human history.

Huston Smith, a religious scholar, wrote in his book *The World's Religions*, "If we take the world's enduring religions at their best, we discover the distilled wisdom of the human race."

This rings true for us. Ancient wisdom tells us that humanity is interdependent. It encourages us to invest in relationships—with ourselves, our family, our neighbors, our world. And it reminds us that creating and cultivating what is good and virtuous is a sacred task.

Yet despite this, our modern relationship with religion is untethered. Starting in the 1990s, the share of Americans who identified with any religion began to drop precipitously—a decline that has been constant and consistent for most of the past 30 years. Those Americans aren't converting to other religions or finding religion later in life. They simply have no religious affiliation whatsoever. This group—nicknamed by many religious scholars as the "Nones"—grew steadily in America, now equaling roughly 30% of the population.

We think it's time to reopen the door to faith and religion as powerful sources of community, transcendence, and social action. The only ideology we are supporting is the *Soul Boom* one: We believe that religions, at a macrolevel, are chapters of humanity's collective story—one that has helped us to evolve and society to gradually (yet not always gracefully) mature.

So we hope you'll work through this section with an open mind and heart and consider that we may have thrown the spiritual baby out with the religious bathwater. We ask you to put your preconceived notions aside and explore what a meaningful relationship with some kind of organized faith tradition might look like for you.

FIELD NOTES!

Interfaith, Then and Now
by Shabnam Mogharabi

It was hot and stuffy inside the women's section of the mosque. I had borrowed a scarf from a basket of head coverings provided for visitors—the fabric smelled strongly of rose-scented perfume and reminded me of my dad's mom, Maman Buzurg, who would visit us from Kelowna, Canada, and massaged floral facial creams into her neck every morning.

The prayers started, and I took my cues from the people around me. Kneel down. Sit up now. I could see the men and boys in the larger room ahead, closer to the altar, under a gold chandelier. I felt a stir of injustice—it seemed unfair that the women were relegated to the back of the mosque in a dimly lit room with painfully little air circulation.

After all, I was the president of the Religious Organizations Council (ROC) at the University of Southern California. We had been invited here to learn more about our Muslim members. And instead, I was seated in the nosebleed section.

"Chill out," I thought. All while I tried not to make eyes at the students seated beside me. (My self-righteous college attitude was firing on all cylinders.)

About 10 minutes later, the prayer service was done, and we walked into the courtyard, with its arched doorways, mosaics, and a small fountain. I hesitated to admit that it was arrestingly beautiful.

The head of the Islamic Student Council came over. "Wasn't that lovely and peaceful?" he asked. I went to open my mouth and unleash my opinions, but my fellow ROC members beat me to it with their nods of agreement. "So nice." "Totally dug it." "The chants were beautiful."

I felt a little taken aback. Had I missed the beauty? I had been so busy thinking about how hot and suffocating and overwhelmingly perfume-y it all was, and how offended the seating arrangement made me feel, that I arrogantly hadn't bothered to pay attention to any part of the prayers. Oops.

Religion is a funny thing. The literal Latin root of the word means "to bind people together, to unite, to create community." Yet more often than not, it's a source of division. Probably because we are all too focused on the predetermined, judgmental voices rattling around in our heads instead of trying to access the spirit behind faith practices with our hearts and souls.

In America, fewer people consider themselves a member of organized religion than ever before. Society largely views it as a negative force—some kind of ancient, irrelevant relic of the past.

Feels like an odd choice to make—to lean away from a meaningful source of community at a time when all signs point to people being more isolated and antisocial and having fewer friends than at any time in recent history.

I've always known spirituality to be important. Vital, even. But it took me a while to realize that some kind of organized faith-based community might be just as grounding. Someone else's doctrine may not be your cup of tea, but perhaps religion still has value in our modern lives.

A decade after my time at USC, I once again found myself on the board of an interfaith organization, the South Coast Interfaith Council. The executive director of the organization, a practicing Muslim, invited the board members to her mosque.

I brought my own (unscented) scarf this time. And as I kneeled in the women's area, I closed my eyes and asked my soul to settle down and pay attention to the ancient beauty of the devotions as they echoed through the air.

And I'm glad I did.

> **Marginal Wisdom**
> "I love you when you bow in your mosque, kneel in your temple, pray in your church. For you and I are sons of one religion, and it is the spirit."
> – Khalil Gibran, philosopher and poet

DEFINE

What does the word "religion" bring to mind for you? Reflect on the origins of your beliefs about a faith practice. What shaped or influenced your beliefs? Family? Cultural traditions? The attitude of friends? What have been your past experiences with religion? Are you still aligned with that background and point of view?

> **Marginal Wisdom**
>
> "This is my simple religion. There is no need for temples; no need for complicated philosophy. Our own brain, our own heart is our temple; the philosophy is kindness."
>
> – Dalai Lama

WRITE

If you ARE a person of faith, what do you get from your practice?
What resonates with you? What comforts you? What do you struggle with in your religion?
If you are NOT a person of faith, what belief system do you subscribe to?
What might you be missing out on without religious ideas?

> **Marginal Wisdom**
>
> "What I know for sure is that if you want to have a grounded life, you've got to have a spiritual foundation. For me, it started with church."
>
> – Oprah Winfrey, TV host and producer

DRAW

Religious trauma is real. *Many people grew up with too-strict morals or judgmentalism in their childhood religious experience. Many cultures create a pressure to adhere to certain faith-based strictures in a way that can feel oppressive. Some families or clergy even wield religion as a weapon of shame. Here's your opportunity to begin to* heal *this trauma. In the box, draw what negative impacts of faith you experienced growing up and explore any unresolved feelings about that as you sketch. Let your imagination and memory express itself in image, picture, line, and color.*

> **Marginal Wisdom**
>
> "We have just enough religion to make us hate, but not enough to make us love one another."
>
> – Jonathan Swift, author

What I wish someone had lovingly relayed to me when I was a child about religion and faith:

_____

_____

_____

_____

ACTIVITY

THE INS & OUTS OF FAITH!

Fill in this "In / Out" table with what you wish were more popular and what you wish would be retired when it comes to different aspects of religion and religious life. We've given you some examples to get you started.

"IN"	"OUT"
• Channeling more Zen into our daily lives	• Using religion to justify violence or war
• Having more compassion for those in need	• Blaming God for your busted tire
• Christian/Country rock song mashups	• Christian/Country rock song mashups
•	•
•	•
•	•
•	•
•	•
•	•
•	•
•	•
•	•
•	•
•	•

Marginal Wisdom

"You are never alone or helpless. The force that guides the stars guides you too."

– Shrii Shrii Anandamurti, philosopher

Section 3: Matters of Faith and Religion

ACTIVITY

RELIGIOUS RITUALS ROUNDUP!

Many of the best parts of the world's various religions are found in their traditions and rituals. In fact, we've sometimes imagined how cool it would be if all these practices cross-pollinated. Maybe all faiths should have a Sabbath—a day of rest when phones are off, prayers are said, and food is shared. How cool would it be if we all took time to bow to the Mecca of our faith traditions five times a day? Or if meditation were woven into our daily lives, as it is in Buddhism?

*Consider this the religious Build-A-Bear of activities! Below is a list of 24 traditions and rituals gathered from across many faiths. Pick the **five** that you wish were universal practices that cross-pollinated into all our lives.*

- **Tonglen Meditation** *Tibetan Buddhism:* A practice of giving and receiving compassion through breath visualization.

- **Sweat Lodge Ceremony** *Indigenous tradition:* A purification ritual involving deep contemplation in an intensely heated sacred space.

- **Sitting Shiva** *Judaism:* A seven-day period of mourning after the burial of a loved one, during which mourners receive visitors for comfort and support.

- **Obon Festival** *Buddhism:* A traditional Japanese communal festival honoring the spirits of your ancestors with food, prayer, and lantern ceremonies.

- **Last Rites** *Christianity:* A sacrament given to those near death to provide them with spiritual healing and forgiveness.

- **Kumbh Mela** *Hinduism:* A mass pilgrimage to bathe in sacred rivers, which must take place every 12 years.

- **Mezuzah** *Judaism:* A small scroll inscribed with Torah verses, affixed to the doorway of a Jewish home, that you touch when entering or exiting to remember God.

- **Baptism** *Christianity:* Ritual immersion in water symbolizing purification and your surrender into a faith.

- **Holi Festival** *Hinduism:* A spring celebration known as the "festival of colors" celebrating love and the start of spring.

- **Festival of Fire** *Zoroastrianism:* A tradition before the first day of spring marked by jumping over fire, leaving sickness behind, and taking in vitality in the new year.

- **Greatest Name Meditation** *Baha'i Faith:* A daily practice of repeating "God is Most Glorious" (Allah'u'abha) 95 times, often while counting prayer beads.

- **Diwali Festival** *Hinduism:* A festival of lights celebration, symbolizing the victory of light over darkness.

- **Elima Ritual** *African Mbuti Efe tribe:* Young women who have their first period move to a special hut for a joyous celebration where they are taught about motherhood and sexual relations as they enter womanhood.

- **Vision Quest** *Indigenous traditions:* An adolescent rite of passage involving solitude and fasting to seek spiritual guidance from the Great Spirit as realized in nature.

- **Ramadan Fasting** *Islam:* Abstaining from food, drink, and other physical needs from dawn to sunset during the ninth month.

- **Bar/Bat Mitzvah** *Judaism:* A coming-of-age commitment ceremony for Jewish boys and girls to mark their maturity and readiness for adulthood.

- **Lent** *Christianity:* A 40-day period of fasting and repentance leading up to Easter.

- **Tilaka Marking** *Hinduism:* Applying a symbolic mark on the forehead to denote devotion or invoke blessings.

- **Sabbath Observance** *Judaism:* A day of rest and spiritual reflection from Friday evening to Saturday evening.

- **Koan Meditation** *Buddhism:* A meditation on paradoxical questions without a direct answer (e.g., "What is the sound of one hand clapping?") in order to open up transcendent thought.

- **Yom Kippur** *Judaism:* A day of atonement marked by fasting and intensive prayer.

- **Salat** *Islam:* Performing a ritualistic prayer five times a day while facing Mecca.

- **Peyote Ceremony** *Indigenous tradition:* Ingesting peyote cactus during spiritual ceremonies for insight, transformation, and initiation.

- **Green Corn Ceremony** *Indigenous tradition:* An annual harvest festival involving dance, fasting, and gratitude.

Below, write out what other rituals, traditions, or sacred ceremonies from other faiths or spiritual practices you admire and might like to experience one day.

> **Marginal Wisdom**
>
> "As your faith is strengthened, you will find that there is no longer the need to have a sense of control, that things will flow as they will, and that you will flow with them, to your great delight and benefit."
>
> – Emmanuel Teney, psychiatrist and Holocaust survivor

ACTIVITY

LOVE QUOTES QUIZ!

*Modern religious debate would have you believe that the world's various faith practices are categorically opposed to each other. But when you read the actual scripture of most faith practices, there are quite a lot of similarities. In fact, we're going to challenge your brain a little. Below are 10 religious or spiritual quotes about one of our most powerful emotions: **LOVE**. Try to match the quote with its source. We have given you one as an example.*

QUOTE ABOUT LOVE

1. "He is the source of love and may be known through love."

2. "Radiate boundless love toward the entire world."

3. "Love is the most great law."

4. "Spread love and peace among yourselves."

5. "Love your neighbor as yourself."

6. "Those who have loved are those that have found God."

7. "To know Love is to know peace."

8. "Let us love one another, for love comes from God. Everyone who loves has been born of God and knows God."

9. "He who loves others is constantly loved by them."

10. "Love others as much as you love yourself. Then you can be entrusted with all things under heaven."

SOURCE

Christianity

Native American Teaching

Taoism

Confucianism

Buddhism

Sikhism

Hinduism

Baha'i Faith

Islam

Judaism

Answer Key: 1 - Hinduism, 2 - Buddhism, 3 - Baha'i Faith, 4 - Islam, 5 - Judaism, 6 - Sikhism, 7 - Native American, 8 - Christianity, 9 - Confucianism, 10 - Taoism.

Soul Boom Workbook: Spiritual Tools for Modern Living

ACTIVITY

Below are 40 core tenets pulled from eight of the world's religious or faith traditions.
Select the **10** tenets that resonate the most with you.

JUDAISM

- **One God**: God is singular, eternal, and the creator of all things.
- **The Torah**: Following God's commandments ensures a righteous life.
- **Tzedakah**: Giving charitably to those in need is a moral duty.
- **Shabbat**: A day of rest and spiritual reflection is sacred.
- **Tikkun Olam**: Humans are responsible for making the world a better place.

BUDDHISM

- **Suffering**: Life has suffering, which arises from craving, but suffering can end.
- **Enlightenment**: Good deeds, words, and thoughts end suffering (lead to Nirvana).
- **Impermanence**: Nothing lasts forever; attachment leads to suffering.
- **No Self**: The soul is not a fixed entity; identity is fluid and ever-changing.
- **Loving-Kindness**: Genuine compassion should extend to all creatures.

CHRISTIANITY

- **Love God**: Develop a deep, personal relationship with God.
- **Love Your Neighbor**: Compassion for others is essential to a righteous life.
- **Jesus as Savior**: A belief in Jesus leads to eternal life and salvation.
- **Forgiveness**: Grace is given to those who show grace and mercy to others.
- **Service**: True greatness comes from humbly serving others.

HINDUISM

- **Dharma**: Everyone has a duty to fill their role in society, to uphold the moral order.
- **Karma**: Actions have consequences and shape destiny, now and in the next life.
- **Moksha**: Life's aim is to attain freedom from the cycle of birth and death.
- **Bhakti**: Devotion to a personal god can help to purify your soul.
- **Ahimsa**: Do not harm any living being in deed, word, or thought.

ISLAM

- **Tawhid**: God is absolute and beyond human comprehension.
- **Salat**: Daily prayer is the only way to maintain a connection with God.
- **Zakat**: A portion of your wealth must be given to help the less fortunate.
- **Sawm**: Fasting purifies the body and strengthens your faith.
- **Hajj**: In your lifetime, take one spiritual pilgrimage to the holy lands.

BAHA'I FAITH

- **Oneness**: People are part of one human family from one Divine Source (one God).
- **Independent Search for Truth**: Each person must seek the truth for themselves.
- **Elimination of Prejudice**: Inequities of race, gender, and class must end.
- **Harmony of Science and Religion**: Faith and reason must align to advance humanity.
- **World Peace**: Peace will only be achieved through justice.

INDIGENOUS FAITH TRADITIONS

- **Interconnectedness**: All life is connected; harming any one part affects the whole.
- **Animism**: Everything has a spirit deserving respect—animals, plants, water, wind.
- **Ancestral Reverence**: Our ancestors guide us, and we must keep their wisdom alive.
- **Sacred Cycles**: Earth has natural rhythms (e.g., moon phases, harvests) that are opportunities for spiritual celebration.
- **Experience over Doctrine**: Spiritual experience comes from dreams, visions, and ceremonies, not scripture.

WICCA (MODERN PAGANISM)

- **The Wiccan Rede**: Pursue your own paths and desires, but do no harm unto others.
- **Reverence for Nature**: Earth is alive, and nature is sacred and must be honored.
- **Dual Divinity**: The feminine and masculine are balanced and in harmony in the form of a God and Goddess.
- **Threefold Law**: Whatever energy (good or bad) that you put into the world will return to you threefold.
- **Ritual Celebration**: Celebrations are timed with the year's natural seasons, solstices, equinoxes, and lunar cycles.

Section 3: Matters of Faith and Religion 51

WRITE

Do you believe you can have a relationship with God without religion or a specific faith tradition? What would that look like? Have you ever felt connected to a Divine Source, but not as part of a religious belief or practice?

Marginal Wisdom

"Men despise religion; they hate it, and fear it is true."

– Blaise Pascal, physicist

EXPLORE

Since the honing of the scientific method and the Age of Reason, people of science and people of faith have engaged in an existential debate: Can discrepancies of faith and reason be resolved or not?

Many scientists view the laws of nature as irreconcilable with faith, believing religion to be an outmoded and outdated superstition that humanity has outgrown. Meanwhile, the faith community distrusts science because their spiritual experiences feel as real as any experiment in a laboratory. Astrophysicist Neil deGrasse Tyson once wrote, "As they are currently practiced, there is no common ground between science and religion ... although just as in hostage negotiations, it's probably best to keep both sides talking to each other." Meanwhile, philosopher and theologian Voltaire said, "Faith consists in believing that which reason does not believe."

Albert Einstein offered a unitive view: "Science without religion is lame; religion without science is blind." Do you agree with Einstein? Why are religion and science so often at odds? How do you think discrepancies of faith and reason can be resolved? Could they simply be two ways of perceiving a singular reality? Do we even need religion and science to agree?

> **Marginal Wisdom**
>
> "Science alone will not save the world. It is through the spiritual connection we feel with nature that we will find the courage and wisdom to make a difference."
>
> – Dr. Jane Goodall, primatologist and conservationist

Section 3: Matters of Faith and Religion

ACTIVITY

HEY KIDS, LET'S INVENT A NEW RELIGION!

In Soul Boom, *we explored religion as a social movement and sought to seek out the similarities between the world's many disparate faiths. But then we took it a step forward and made up a new religion called (you guessed it!)* SoulBoom, the Religion™. *It wasn't meant to be heretical, and it was somewhat in jest, but the intention was sincere: to identify and define what we believed an "ideal" and universal faith practice could look like. Below is a recap of our* **SoulBoom, the Religion** *framework. Take a look through its principles and reflect on them. Then, we encourage you to imagine a religion that works for you.*

There are some foundational similarities that bind most world religions together. **SoulBoom, the Religion,** *believes in these 10 fundamentals of all faith traditions:*

- A Higher Power
- Life After Death
- The Power of Prayer
- Transcendence
- Community
- A Moral Compass
- The Force of Love
- Increased Compassion
- Service to the Poor
- Strong Sense of Purpose

In SoulBoom, the Religion, we proposed specifically including these 10 additional principles:

- No Clerics
- Diversity Plus Harmony
- Centrality of the Divine Feminine
- Cooperation of Science and Faith
- Connection to the Natural World
- Centrality of Justice
- A Life of Service
- Practical Spiritual Tools
- Emphasis on Music and Arts
- Humility
- *Bonus:* Potlucks!

YOUR TURN!

My new religion is called _____

Core Principles:

_____   _____
_____   _____
_____   _____
_____   _____
_____   _____
_____   _____
_____   _____

Soul Boom Workbook: Spiritual Tools for Modern Living

Create a symbol or emblem for your faith that resonates with you and expresses its essence.
Draw it here.

Marginal Wisdom

"True Islam taught me that it takes all of the religious, political, economic, psychological, and racial ingredients, or characteristics, to make the human family... complete."

– Malcolm X, Muslim civil rights leader and activist

What would it feel like to experience your religion?
How would believers engage with this faith and its rituals and practices?

_____
_____
_____
_____
_____
_____
_____

PAUSE & PONDER

You made it through the first (and possibly the most existential) of all the parts of the Soul Boom Workbook.

In this first unit, we dug deep into the biggest, most profound words (and all the stigmas associated with them) that arise during a spiritual journey: soul, spirituality, God, faith, religion. You wrote, drew, and, we hope, experienced moments of deep reflection.

Take a minute to flip back through the pages of Part One. Below, reflect on your journey thus far.

What was your favorite writing prompt, reflection, or activity? Why? What did it reveal about yourself?

Which prompt, reflection, or activity was the most challenging for you or made you the most uncomfortable? Why do you think that is?

As you head into the next part, which explores how spirituality shapes your personal ideology, what are your biggest takeaways from this unit of work?

Draw, doodle, or sketch any final images that pop into your head as you move forward on your spiritual journey.

USE THIS SPACE TO CONTINUE EXPLORING!

Part

TWO

Section 5:
Meditation, Contemplation, and Reflection

Section 6:
The Power of Prayer

Section 4:
Sacred Spaces

Section 7:
Values, Virtues, and Morality

Section 8:
Beauty, Nature, and Art

Your Personal Soul Boom

In Which We Get Contemplative

Section 4

SACRED SPACES

ON any given day in our modern lives, the same things take up most of the real estate in our minds—schedules, appointments, deadlines, school, work, meetings, notifications, Netflix, memes, and bills. And everyone's favorite question: What should we have delivered for dinner? Then it's time to pass out and start the whole process all over again tomorrow.

The Buddhists call this static in our brain space the monkey mind.

But there are numerous mind-expanding, reality-changing, soul-shaking concepts that we rarely (if ever) allow any meaningful space. That's the point of this section (and the next few) of the *Soul Boom Workbook*.

In Part One, we asked you to dig into the foundation of your belief system and define the principal terms that are must-haves for any soul quest—spirituality, religion, God. Now in Part Two, we want you to contemplate all the ideas that make up your *personal* spiritual life—what *you* hold sacred, how *your* soul communicates, ways *you* commune with creation, and what it really means when *you* worship.

This is the big, meaty stuff that enriches and shapes our inner lives. Prayer. Morality. Beauty. And we're starting with a rare but crucial one: sacredness. Oft forgotten in the buzz and bubble of the modern world.

Spiritual journeys can take us in many directions and enrich our lives in multiple ways. However, we must begin by turning inward—connecting to the source—and recognizing our true inner natures. Focusing on this underused, underappreciated concept of the sacred—especially given the sacredness of our own souls—is a great place to start this journey. From there, our definitions can expand outward.

Joni Mitchell sang in "Big Yellow Taxi": *"Don't it always seem to go / That you don't know what you've got 'til it's gone / They paved paradise and put up a parking lot."*

We don't want the sacred in our lives to be lost forever. So before your brain becomes a parking lot of to-do lists, Zooms, and nonstop scrolling, let's reclaim the beauty and paradise of the sacred. Let's slow down our monkey minds. Let's think through and identify the things that you believe are worth venerating and reflect on what they mean to your heart.

FIELD NOTES!

The Sacred Hallway
by Rainn Wilson

The most sacred place I can possibly think of is a drab hallway, lit by flickering fluorescent lights and lined by folding chairs, in the back of a crappy hospital in Van Nuys, California.

Why? Because that is where my wife and son *almost* died during childbirth.

After the 2 a.m. hemorrhaging and the ambulance and even more bleeding and no available rooms and the nurse being unable to find my son's heartbeat and my wife being placed on a bed in the hallway and the staff being unable to reach our doctor on his pager and the five units of blood lost and the cord wrapped around our baby's little neck and the panic and prayers, Dr. Foroohar burst into the delivery room at 4 a.m., bellowing for a C-section, and successfully cut young Walter McKenzie Wilson out of his traumatized mother's womb.

Holiday Reinhorn, my wife, overcame pain and terror with a power that was greater than that of any Marvel superhero.

When she was, thankfully, pronounced stable, and three-minute-old Walter was brought to my trembling arms in that same hallway, and I gazed into his bright blue eyes, I felt God, the universe, meaning, hope, life, and energy in a way I never have before or since.

You see, sacred doesn't need to mean a church or shrine or holy relic or monument. Sacred can mean linoleum and aluminum chairs and chipped paint and the smell of Lysol at four in the morning.

Sacred can be an action and not just a place. It can mean the *sacrifice* (notice the Latin root word "sacer," meaning "holy," in both) that women like Holiday make to carry the children of Planet Earth and bring them—painfully, dramatically, and with a miraculous explosion of love and guts—into the world.

Holy is what we make it. How we experience it. And it can heal our society, too! The concept of preserving and honoring something sacred is a force that can unite folks on all sides of any political, ideological, or religious spectrum.

For some, nature is sacred. For some, it might be an altar. To part of the population, the awe and miracle of the cosmos evoke a holy magic. For others, it might be a battlefield where many brave men lost their lives. For some, it's the right of self-expression; for others, it's the right to worship that is most revered.

In *Soul Boom: Why We Need a Spiritual Revolution*, I wrote at great length about my pilgrimage to Haifa, and Akka, Israel, and visiting the holiest sites in the Baha'i world. I sought to evoke the profound feelings that blossomed in my heart, and the profound meaning that the prayerful trip brought up in me. And I explored how and why it's so difficult to tap into what is consecrated in our mundane daily lives.

But the thing is, you don't need to visit holy shrines to create a pilgrimage. When I took 12-year-old Walter to visit my childhood homes and schools and trees and playgrounds in Olympia, and Shoreline, Washington, that, too, was a kind of divinely inspired journey.

The swing set at Westside Elementary School where I lost my last tooth. The parking lot at Shorecrest High School where I asked my first girlfriend out on a date. (Walter: "Ew, Dad.") These were sacred sites for me, in their way. Sharing them with my son had a kind of mysterious power.

It's challenging to find what is sacred in the modern world. I live north of suburban Los Angeles, and there are an awful lot of dumpsters and freeway on-ramps and donut shops and endless power lines decorating the horizon here. Can any of those things really be holy?

In this section of our workbook, we will aspire to help you determine your sacred spaces. Your divine connections. It may be the touchpoint where your spiritual journey launches. We implore you to dive deep!

For me, a visit to that particular Van Nuys hospital hallway may now be impossible, but Holiday and I hold its terrifying holiness in our hearts, and we will until the day we die. Maybe that's what it's all about.

> **Marginal Wisdom**
>
> "I felt in need of a great pilgrimage, so I sat still for three days, and God came to me."
>
> – Kabir, 15th-century poet

DEFINE

Some people associate sacredness with stillness or quiet. Others with natural beauty and some with a place of worship. Below is the dictionary definition of "sacred."

> **sacred** *adjective* [sa•cred]
>
> dedicated or set apart for the service or worship of a deity;
> devoted exclusively to one practice;
> worthy of religious veneration

Now, write your own, more modern definition of the word "sacred."
Consider including all the words, phrases, or ideas that you associate with sacredness.

sacred *adjective* [sa•cred] _____

_____

_____

_____

Marginal Wisdom

"The work of the eyes is done. Go now and do the heart-work on the images imprisoned within you. That is sacred."

– Rainer Maria Rilke, poet

DRAW

Close your eyes and imagine what sacred looks like to you. What was the first image that popped in your mind? Was it a landscape? A beautiful object? A temple? An experience with loved ones? Something special from your adolescence? Draw that "something sacred" below.

> **Marginal Wisdom**
>
> "Your sacred space is where you can find yourself over and over again."
>
> – Joseph Campbell, author and religious scholar

Section 4: Sacred Spaces

REFLECT

Describe some of the familial, cultural, or faith-based rituals, gatherings, ceremonies, or experiences that you had during your childhood that mean the most to your heart and memory. Do you still practice any of them? If not, do you miss them? Why? What draws you to those memories?

_____

_____

_____

_____

_____

_____

_____

_____

_____

_____

_____

_____

_____

How does excavating them affect or touch you? Would you consider bringing them back into your adult life in some way?

Marginal Wisdom

"It is necessary to go back to seeing the family as sacred — 'the heart of the culture of life.'"

– Pope St. John Paul II

_____

_____

_____

_____

_____

_____

_____

_____

_____

_____

EXPLORE

In Soul Boom, Rainn wrote of his Baha'i pilgrimage to Haifa, Israel, and compared it to the pilgrimage many football fans make to places like Lambeau Field in Green Bay, Wisconsin. What do you think makes something feel sacred? Are objects like a crucifix or places like Stonehenge sacred because some ancient human or religion decided they were? Because they hung a plaque there telling us it is sacred?

Or is it possible to have a sacred space that is sacred only to you? Meaning, is it possible to "sacralize" a place yourself? Does it need to have some kind of group consensus? Or can some things just be intrinsically sacred? Reflect on your thoughts below.

> **Marginal Wisdom**
>
> "I now believe that whether or not there's a God, there is such a thing as sacredness. Life is sacred. The Sabbath can be a sacred day. Prayer can be a sacred ritual. There is something transcendent, beyond the everyday. It's possible that humans created this sacredness ourselves, but that doesn't take away from its power or importance."
>
> – A. J. Jacobs, in *The Year of Living Biblically*

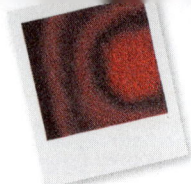

ACTIVITY

SACRED PHOTO SWAP!

Ready? Here's what we want you to do:

1. Take a photo of something or somewhere that is sacred to you.
2. Send the picture to someone you love and tell them why it's sacred to you.
3. Ask them to send you a picture of what is sacred to them.
4. Explore your experience below.

What photo did you choose and why?

> **Marginal Wisdom**
>
> "Wherever we may come alive, that is the area in which we are spiritual."
>
> – David Steindl-Rast, Benedictine monk and author

Whom did you send it to? Why that person?

How did they respond? How did sharing it make you feel?

68 Soul Boom Workbook: Spiritual Tools for Modern Living

ACTIVITY

YOUR SACRED TREE!

For many Indigenous peoples, it is impossible to separate the sacred from nature. The two go inexorably hand in hand. Mountain, lake, river, rock, plant, animal. Each contains a spirit of sacredness and its own individual mythology, elevating the natural world to the state of the divine. Jewell Praying Wolf James, a Lummi Nation leader and author, once said: "If we can't protect the Earth, can't protect the sky; if we can't protect our sacred sites, then we've failed the world."

We want to participate in this gratitude for nature. Find a tree near your home. One that you like. Set a timer for 10 minutes and observe it completely. Notice every knot in the bark, the shapes of the leaves, the animals and insects that call it home. This is now your sacred tree. Check back in with it every week for the next three months. Notice its changes. Speak to it. Commune with it. Yes, you can even occasionally hug it. Reflect on your experience.

Describe your tree on Day One: _____

Month One observations: _____

> **Marginal Wisdom**
>
> "This mountain has my heart. This land is our church."
>
> – Caleen Sisk, chief of the Winnemem Wintu tribe

Month Two observations: _____

Month Three observations: _____

Section 4: Sacred Spaces   69

ACTIVITY

MY SACRED VISION BOARD!

Let's create a big, beautiful, dynamic visual reminder to help you implement more sacredness into your daily life. Pull out a big piece of construction or poster paper. Build out a collage or creative visual snapshot of all that you find sacred and all that you want to regularly reference. As you build out your sacredness vision board masterpiece, consider including or incorporating some of the suggestions below. Then, fill the margins with doodles of the myriad things that lift your heart.

A simple ritual you can do every day to connect with the divine.

A handwritten prayer or affirmation that resonates with you.

A timeline of your one sacred life, noting all the moments where you felt connected to the greater world.

An envelope labeled "Sacred Secrets" where you can tuck little notes about the things closest to your heart and soul that you aren't ready to share with others yet.

A playlist of song titles that bring you peace or joy every time you hear them.

A space for an image or sketch of your sacred tree from *every season*.

At least three quotes that inspire you.

Printed photos of people, places, experiences, or things that are blessed to you.

A photo of you as a child to remind you of the sacredness of our inner lives.

A sketch or description of a place in your house that becomes a shrine for something meaningful to you.

Marginal Wisdom

"The sacredness of life is not in the object, but in the process."

– Lailah Gifty Akita, author and youth advocate

A color palette or swatches that represent your spiritual energy.

A poem or song lyric that speaks to your soul.

A phrase in another language that connects to your cultural roots.

Section 4: Sacred Spaces   71

ACTIVITY

MY ULTIMATE SACRED SPACE!

Imagine you are asked to design a sacred space, a place that appeals to the holy impulse in everyone. When architect Siamak Hariri was asked to do just that—submit a design for a Baha'i temple in Chile, one that would be open to people of all countries, backgrounds, and belief systems—he thought a lot about what the edifice should convey.

In his viral TED Talk, Hariri says, "I loved this idea of the inner and the outer, like when you see someone and you say, 'That person is radiant.' And I was thinking, 'My gosh, how could we make something architectural out of that, where you create a building and it becomes alive with light?'"

The model (left image) of the temple he submitted played with the idea of incarnate light and the unity of the inner and outer spirit. Hariri's design was ultimately selected, and the temple was eventually constructed. The final structure is below (right image).

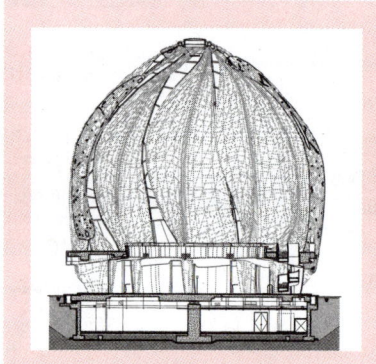 

Now, it's your turn to design a sacred space, one that appeals to your soul. Fill in the following build plan and set the parameters for how you want this place to look, feel, and flow.

Name your space: _____

Where is it located? _____

Write an intention for your space: _____

_____

_____

_____

I want to use my sacred space for:

☐ Meditation   ☐ Creativity   ☐ Clarity   ☐ Healing
☐ Reflection   ☐ Celebration   ☐ Courage   ☐ Joy
☐ Prayer   ☐ Peace   ☐ Mourning   ☐ Time in Nature
☐ Other: _____

MY SACRED SPACE'S BUILD SPECS:

Dimensions: _____ x _____ x _____

Colors: _____

Building Materials (e.g., stone, brick, glass): _____

Textures (e.g., soft, natural, wood): _____

Sounds (e.g., silent, soft music, guided meditations): _____

Scents (e.g., none, candles, fresh flowers, incense): _____

Furnishings (e.g., cushions, lighting, plants): _____

Decorations (e.g., art, rugs, paint): _____

What you want a visitor using your sacred space to feel or experience:

_____

_____

Sketch your sacred space below. Fill it with as much joy, light, and details as you can!

> **Marginal Wisdom**
>
> "Do you not know that you are God's temple and that God's Spirit dwells in you?"
>
> – The Bible
> (1 Corinthians 3:16)

Section 4: Sacred Spaces

Section 5

MEDITATION, CONTEMPLATION, and REFLECTION

PICTURE this: You're deep in a jungle in India thousands of years ago. The air is thick. Nobody is texting. No plastic water bottles litter the forest floor. There's just a big old fig tree and a young man sitting underneath it. His eyes are closed. He is still.

Then, just before dawn, the man opens his eyes. He has done it. He understands it all—what suffering is and how to end it. He understands how to achieve bliss. He is "awakened."

The man is the Buddha. And what do you imagine this 35-year-old who has just achieved enlightenment decides to do? Drink champagne? Take a bath? Tell his best friend?

Nope.

The Buddha decides to keep meditating. He has achieved liberation from the self, and he chooses to stay put under the Bodhi tree, meditating for seven more days.

If you think that's wild, in Japan, there are monks who do a 1,000-day walking meditation over the course of seven years as part of their practice and training. That's a lot of stillness and time in your own mind. And bunions!

The truth is, meditation has been around as long as humans have. Its practitioners believe that meditation is capable of helping us achieve a state of profound, blissful contemplation—what the Buddhists call *samadhi*. (Samadhi is also described as a state of deep absorption, where the mind is still, yet fully alert and aware.) This transcendence is the end game for many when it comes to meditation.

Today, the meditation buffet is massive: mantra-based, breath-focused, heart-opening, scripture-soaked, candle-staring, body-scanning, dishwashing-enlightenment kind of stuff. Or just sitting and doing absolutely nothing . . . on purpose. Yet even with this variety, it can be hard to find the time or motivation to explore meditation. Luckily, our phone, while often a distraction, can actually be a tool to unlock this mind magic. There are apps—like Headspace, Calm, Insight Timer, Sol—that offer guided, bite-sized ways to get a handle on this ancient practice.

There are also numerous inspiring guides, books, and audio tools for meditation and its practices, if that's more your speed. We don't have room for all of them in this tiny section of our book. So instead, we want to ask you to reflect on what serenity and clarity could look like in your life. We want to encourage you to engage in peaceful contemplation and to give you a few introductory and out-of-the-box ideas to begin your mindfulness* journey.

*Note: We're not huge fans of the term "mindfulness." The mind is so often the source of angst, misery, and static that we prefer the concept of "heartfulness" or even "breathfulness" as a hook to hang our contemplation on.

The physiological benefits to a regular meditation practice are numerous. Positive psychology researchers have shown that even five minutes of meditation a day are incredibly effective at reducing anxiety and depression, lowering blood pressure, and improving focus, sleep, health, and well-being.

Everyone's favorite poet to quote Mary Oliver says, "Attention is the beginning of devotion." In its simplest form, meditation is simply training the mind to pay attention. It's a tool you can pull from your sacred tool belt and practice anywhere, anytime.

And the spiritual and health benefits are legendary.

FIELD NOTES!

Notes from My Monkey Mind
by Shabnam Mogharabi

My anxiety was on high alert. I had spent the past four months on a roadshow, taking meetings with more than 50 different companies, VCs, strategic funds, and high-net-worth individuals. At one point, I was forced to kindly nudge one billionaire out of our office after a two-hour long conversation so I could get to a meeting with the next billionaire who was waiting on a Zoom. True story.

My end game was to raise a Series B round for SoulPancake, the media company I had cofounded with Rainn. (We have known each other a very long time.) The meetings were running on autopilot—I had mastered extolling the company's virtues, summing up our profitable numbers, singing the praises of our team, all while exuding smarts, confidence, and charm.

I was killing it . . . on the outside.

But my brain? It was an avalanche of rapid-fire thoughts: *If so-and-so hasn't responded to the follow-up to my first follow-up, should I take the hint and move on? Should I be worried that there are no women on this company's board? How many cups of coffee have I had today? Is a strategic partner a safer bet, or a disaster waiting to happen? How will the upcoming election affect the media industry? Will I ever have* time to go on a date again? Are my spidey senses off, or is this team way too eager to make a deal happen? Am I failing my staff? Did I even sleep last night?

The truth is, this mind-scatter was messing me up. I was doing the things I needed to do on autopilot. But I was unfocused and drained. I wasn't present with family and friends. I remember one of my best friends told me at the time, "You're not here ... so if you need to go, just go." (Damn, that one made me feel guilty.) I was run, run, running on the fundraising wheel, with no space for calm, peace, or slowing down in my life. It was as if who I was had been co-opted by the chaos of my thoughts.

I was telling one of our company advisors about how much anxiety had built up about this process, and she suggested I pick up a meditation practice. At the time, the Calm app was just making waves, so I signed up for a three-month subscription.

Every morning, while I was applying mascara or making a soft-boiled egg, I tried to clear my mind and listen. To focus on the soothing, feminine voice on the app and shut down the endless spiral of worries in my brain. Yet every morning, this practice felt foreign ... I just didn't get it. And I'd stop the guided meditation halfway through and race out the door. (I clearly missed the memo that you can't multitask your way to meditative bliss.) This happened for nearly a month.

It didn't matter. Although the outcome of the investment raise was beyond my control, it ultimately worked out. We ended up selling the company. Not what we expected, but better than we could have imagined.

What didn't work out as well after our acquisition was my inner state. I came out on the other side of the process into an exciting new chapter for our company and team. I also came out with a mind that didn't feel any more connected or clear. My lack of energy and disengagement with the present moment was still there. It just found new things to focus on.

It took several years before I figured out what is actually effective for me in wrestling back control of my mind ... and my life. For one thing, I've learned that guided audio meditations and visualizations don't do it for me. What does work is nature. Fresh air. Music. Box breathing.

My meditation practice circa 2016 did not get me the quick kumbaya I was seeking. These days, especially since having kids (who require one to be present in oh-so-many other ways), I view my meditative and contemplative practice completely differently. It involves walks before dinner with my dog. It includes moments of peace in the park and the nature trail near my home. It involves music playing in my ears and drowning out all other sounds. Footsteps felt on the ground. Leaves rustling. Standing in the sun. Deep, calming breaths. And, in a lot of ways, radical acceptance of the way my brain works.

It may not be conventional ... and there's certainly no app for it ... but it's working for me.

> **Marginal Wisdom**
>
> "It's like having a charger for your whole body and mind. That's what meditation is!"
>
> – Jerry Seinfeld, comedian and actor

DEFINE

Today, meditation is fairly easy to define and universally understood. Instead, let's dig into what your past experiences with meditation have been like. Have you ever tried meditating? When? For how long? What was the experience like? What did you enjoy about it, and what made it hard for you? Write about your relationship with the practice of meditation and the challenges that come with it.

> **Marginal Wisdom**
>
> "Meditation is the only time I have encountered my own mind and thought, 'Wow. This could use a little work.'"
>
> – Elizabeth Gilbert, journalist and author

EXPLORE

One of the most challenging aspects of meditation can be determining how to build a personal practice. So let's explore your goals here. What would you like to get from a meditation practice? What issues might it help you navigate? If meditation were able to unlock greater focus and clarity, how do you think that might elevate your life and work? If it were able to inspire greater connection, meaning, and inner peace, how do you think that might inspire your life's path?

> **Marginal Wisdom**
>
> "Your inner voice is the voice of divinity. To hear it, we need to be in solitude, even in crowded places."
>
> – A. R. Rahman, composer and music producer

ACTIVITY

WELCOME TO YOUR MEDITATION PRIMER!

MY MEDITATIVE WEEK!

This activity aims to ease you into meditation with simple reflections. Every day of this week, select one of the meditations listed below to try out. Then, log which one you did and your observations on it in the calendar. Easy, right? Get to it.

*These are the seven meditations to choose from.
Do them in any order that you'd like.*

THE ONE-MINUTE BREATHER

Meditation doesn't have to be long! Set a 60-second timer on your phone. Relax your shoulders. Unclench your jaw. Close your eyes. Focus on your breathing. How it goes into the lungs. How it fills your soft belly. How it feels coming out of your mouth. There is only this moment. Pay attention for one minute.

THE WALK

Find a place where you can safely wander. Take slow, intentional steps. Feel the air move into your nostrils and out of your mouth. Pay attention to the sound and feel of each footstep you take. Notice and send love to the leaves, grass, light, and all else around you. Be present.

THE BODY SCAN

Set an alarm for five minutes. Settle into a chair. Imagine you are an MRI machine. Starting at the crown of your head, inch down your body. Stop at any organ, joint, or feature you'd like along the way. Check in on it. Is it tense? Release it. Thank it for its role in your life. Continue down until you reach your feet.

THE HANDHOLD

Clasp your own hands gently, either in your lap or over your heart. Notice the texture of your skin, the warmth in your palms, the pressure of your fingers. Let this small act of self-comfort soothe you. Breathe in and out six times as you focus on the sensation of being held, even by yourself.

THE LIGHT CATCHER

Sit in a spot where light can find you. Ideally a window or standing in a sunbeam outside. But a lamp will do, too. Stay there for at least five minutes. Feel the light on your skin. Visualize the light moving through you, warming you. Imagine it creating a soft glow inside you. Soak it in.

THE HEARTBEAT

Place your fingers lightly on your wrist, neck, or chest. Find your heartbeat. Focus your attention on it. Notice its rhythm. Appreciate its strength. With each beat, silently say to yourself, "I am alive, I am alive, I am alive" until the words and the heartbeat blur together in your mind. Let that be enough.

THE SOUNDTRACK

Take a seat anywhere. Close your eyes and bring attention to your ears. Collect the sounds around you. Notice what is loudest, then what is softest. Is there a hum? A car passing by? A child playing? The sound of your own breath? Each is part of this moment. Do not think—just listen and notice.

Soul Boom Workbook: Spiritual Tools for Modern Living

MONDAY

Today's Meditation:

How It Felt:

TUESDAY

Today's Meditation:

How It Felt:

WEDNESDAY

Today's Meditation:

How It Felt:

THURSDAY

Today's Meditation:

How It Felt:

FRIDAY

Today's Meditation:

How It Felt:

> **Marginal Wisdom**
>
> "Meditation is not a way of making your mind quiet. It's a way of entering into the quiet that's already there—buried under the 50,000 thoughts the average person thinks every day."
>
> – Deepak Chopra, physician, philosopher, and author

SATURDAY

Today's Meditation:

How It Felt:

SUNDAY

Today's Meditation:

How It Felt:

Section 5: Meditation, Contemplation, and Reflection

WARNING: FREESTYLE DRAWING AHEAD!

ACTIVITY

MINDFULNESS DOODLE!

This is not *about being a great artist or achieving anything on the page. We are simply tapping into the feeling and motion of drawing. Set a timer for five minutes. Ensure your space is quiet and free of distractions. Perhaps put on music. Now, with a deep exhale, begin to let your pen move across the paper in random shapes and patterns. Notice the sound of the pen on the paper. Move your pen (or pencil) with the rhythm of your breath. Go with the flow and don't worry about results. Try shapes, free-flowing lines, patterns, and loops. Fill the page. Bring your meditative drawing to life!*

Marginal Wisdom

"Soon silence will have passed into legend. Man has turned his back on silence. Day after day, he invents machines and devices that increase noise and distract humanity from the essence of life, contemplation, meditation."

– Jean Arp, artist

★ BONUS ★

Did you enjoy this exercise? Make it a regular part of your exploration into mindfulness!
Buy a tablet of quality art paper and a nice set of pens.
Set aside time every night for your meditative doodling.

WRITE

We know ... schedules are busy. Life moves quickly. And most days flash by in an instant. But ancient wisdom tells us introspection is important. Where and when during your day or week can you carve out dedicated time for self-reflection? What would need to happen for you to find time for this? Describe the place and time circumstances you would need to create in order to make your meditation resonate.

> **Marginal Wisdom**
> "Half an hour's meditation each day is essential, except when you are busy. Then a full hour is needed."
>
> – Francis de Sales, Catholic saint

ACTIVITY

**IDEA!
NO SPECIAL CIRCUMSTANCES ARE NEEDED!**

MEDITATE THE MUNDANE!

Being present—fully, entirely present—in each moment of life is often considered an intentional and mindful act. Consider this passage from Buddhist monk and peace activist Thich Nhat Hanh:

"If while washing dishes, we think only of the cup of tea that awaits us, thus hurrying to get the dishes out of the way as if they were a nuisance, then we are not 'washing the dishes to wash the dishes.' What's more, we are not alive during the time we are washing the dishes. In fact, we are completely incapable of realizing the miracle of life while standing at the sink. If we can't wash the dishes, the chances are we won't be able to drink our tea either. While drinking the cup of tea, we will only be thinking of other things, barely aware of the cup in our hands. Thus we are sucked away into the future—and we are incapable of actually living one minute of life."

Marginal Wisdom

"Zen does not confuse spirituality with thinking about God while one is peeling potatoes. Zen spirituality is just to peel the potatoes."

– Alan Watts, author

Now it's your turn to find contemplation in the mundane. Pick an ordinary household task (e.g., doing laundry). Start the task and focus completely on it while taking deep, slow breaths. Pay attention to how your hands move, the sounds of the chore, the textures you're feeling. Notice when and how often your mind wanders . . . and where it wanders to. Gently and with humor and acceptance, ask your mind to come on back and be present with the task at hand. Try this a few times this month. Who knows; someday, you might just look forward to folding fitted sheets!

84 *Soul Boom Workbook: Spiritual Tools for Modern Living*

ACTIVITY

CHOOSE YOUR OWN (REFLECTIVE) ADVENTURE!

*Select **one** of the three activities below that encourage introspection. Consider choosing the one that makes you the most uncomfortable or seems the hardest—it may be the one you most need to experience. Do the activity, then write about it below.*

Affirmation Station

Find a place in your house that you pass by several times a day (e.g., the closet door, bathroom mirror, your refrigerator). Think of something you're feeling a "negative" emotion about—anger, frustration, disappointment, sadness. Write an affirmation on a Post-it note that validates and accepts the emotion. Put it in your affirmation spot. Every time you see the note, repeat the affirmation 10 times. Do this for 5 days.

Brain Broadcast

Find a mirror and stand in front of it. Have a brave conversation out loud with yourself about the things in your life that you need clarity on. What choices are you struggling with? What in your life could use more time for reflection? What are you afraid will happen if you make the wrong choices? (Note: Do this alone, lest someone question your sanity.)

Be in Your Body

Think about something you're presently struggling with. Now, find a private space with a comfortable rug. Set a 10-minute timer. Turn on some music (or don't) and lie down on the ground. Reflect on your emotions and try to experience the feelings in and with your body. With your eyes closed, come to life on the floor. Let your body stretch, express, shake, and gesticulate in ways that you perhaps never have before. Shut off your mind and brain and allow movement to flow freely. Move past your self-conscience and let your body call the shots.

> **Marginal Wisdom**
>
> "Everyone should find some suitable time, day or night, to sink into his depths, each according to his own fashion."
>
> – Johannes Tauler, mystic and author

Which experience did you choose, and why? As you were doing the exercise, did any part of it feel challenging? How did you feel after you completed it? What felt good? What didn't? Reflect on the activity below. Consider going back and trying the others at a later time.

_____
_____
_____
_____
_____
_____
_____

Section 5: Meditation, Contemplation, and Reflection

ACTIVITY

REFLECT ON YOUR RUMINATIONS!

Reflection is not the same thing as rumination. Rumination is a negative thought pattern where the mind hyper-focuses on an upsetting past event or an unlikely future outcome. Sometimes described casually as overthinking, it's kind of like watching a shoe go around in a dryer. Sometimes we can spend much of our days in this state! So we've created this helpful tool to help all the ruminators out there. One that guides you from unhealthy rumination toward healthy contemplation. (For some women, this can be a useful exercise, as research indicates that women are two times more likely than men to ruminate on their worries.) Writing it out can be quite helpful, too! Feel free to make copies of these pages and use them any time your brain just won't shut up about something.

THE RUMINATION REFLECTION WORKSHEET

What's on your mind? Right now, I keep incessantly thinking about:

_____
_____
_____

What's bothering you most about it? What's most frustrating/confusing/difficult is:

_____
_____
_____

How does this make you feel (really)? Every time this pops into my mind, I feel:

_____
_____
_____

And in my body, I notice: _____

_____
_____
_____

What's the story you're telling yourself? The narrative running around in my head is:

_____
_____
_____
_____

What do you know to be true? Some objective truths and facts (not feelings!) are:

_____
_____
_____
_____

What are you most afraid might happen? If this doesn't turn out how I want, I fear:

_____
_____
_____
_____

What is actually within your control about this?
One thing I can focus my attention on is:

_____
_____
_____
_____

> **Marginal Wisdom**
>
> "When we're lost in thought—especially if we're ruminating—it's like we're in a trance. Meditation wakes us up from that."
>
> – Tara Brach, psychologist, author, and meditation teacher

What would you say to a friend who couldn't stop ruminating? I would tell my friend:

_____
_____
_____
_____

Pop star Cher once said, "If it doesn't matter in five years, it doesn't matter."
Consider this for yourself now. My older, wiser self would say the outcome here is:

_____
_____
_____
_____

ACTIVITY

REFLECTION QUOTES QUIZ!

The ability to reflect and contemplate on our lives, choices, actions, and the world around us is an incredibly powerful tool. It's one that every spiritual practice in the world affirms as vital to our well-being, especially when that meditative energy is directed toward understanding the divine. Below are 10 quotes from various faith practices about meditation and reflection. See if you can match the quote to its source. We have given you one as an example.

QUOTE ABOUT REFLECTION

1. "Meditate on God's name and you shall obtain all treasures."

2. "The soul has five levels . . . each deeper than the last, and meditation allows us to access these inner dimensions."

3. "But his delight is in the law of the Lord, and on His law he meditates day and night."

4. "Meditation brings wisdom; lack of meditation leaves ignorance. Know well what leads you forward and what holds you back, and choose the path that leads to wisdom."

5. "To the mind that is still, the whole universe surrenders."

6. "Deep within us all there is an amazing inner sanctuary of the soul, a holy place . . . to which we may continuously return."

7. "Meditate profoundly, that the secret of things unseen may be revealed unto you."

8. "There is a polish for everything that takes away rust; and the polish for the heart is the remembrance of God."

9. "A reflective, contented mind is the best possession."

10. "Can you hear the mountain? Can you hear the pine tree? Can you hear the wind? They all speak. Are you listening?"

SOURCE

Islam

Taoism

Sikhism

Quakerism

Kabbalah (Jewish Mysticism)

Baha'i Faith

Buddhism

First Nations prayer

Christianity

Zoroastrianism

1 - Sikhism, 2 - Kabbalah, 3 - Christianity, 4 - Buddhism, 5 - Taoism, 6 - Quakerism, 7 - Baha'i Faith, 8 - Islam, 9 - Zoroastrianism, 10 - First Nations

Soul Boom Workbook: Spiritual Tools for Modern Living

DRAW

In the Bible, it is written, "But when you pray, go into your inner room, close the door and pray to your Father who is in secret." (Matthew 6:6). We love the idea that we all have an inner room, a place away from the crazy of our lives and the world around us! A space that we can go to, close the door, and commune with the divine—pray, meditate, contemplate, and be still. In the space below, draw what you envision your "inner room" to look like. What does this personal sanctum of peace, prayer, and purpose look like in your mind's eye?

> **Marginal Wisdom**
>
> "Meditation is to dive all the way within, beyond thought, to the source of thought and pure consciousness.... When you come out, you come out refreshed, filled with energy and enthusiasm for life."
>
> – David Lynch, filmmaker

Section 6

The
POWER
of
PRAYER

WE at *Soul Boom* offer this prayer for humanity:

> *Dear God or Universe or Great Spirit,*
> *May we live and act with compassion. May we protect what is sacred—each other, our planet, and the truth. May we always seek to first understand. May we allow our choices to be courageous. May we be guided by love, justice, and peace. And may we never forget that we belong to one shared human family.*

How did it make you feel to read that? Did you think, "That was nice"? Did it warm your heart? Did you instinctively want to say "Amen" or "Shalom" or another religious closing? Or did you feel a little uncomfortable because prayer has always seemed a little weird to you?

According to the 2020 World Values Study, more than 50% of people globally pray at least a few times per week—in America, 44% of people say they pray daily, according to the Pew Research Center. And while membership in organized religion has declined, a third of the people with no religious affiliation at all still report praying on occasion.

This makes sense to us. Prayer is one of the most powerful tools at our disposal for self-expression. Prayer enriches our inner spiritual lives. It can be deeply personal. And science shows that prayer is also wildly good for our mental well-being. A large population study conducted by Harvard University and published in the *American Journal of Epidemiology* in 2018 found that young adults who prayed daily were less likely to be depressed and have higher levels of life satisfaction and self-esteem than those who never prayed.

But people also have a lot of deeply held assumptions about prayer. Some feel that prayer needs to be intrinsically religious in nature. That it only works if you have unwavering faith or believe in some kind of Sky-Daddy figure.

Others believe that prayer has to be said in a certain way, using certain words. After all, prayers should always be calm and polite, never angry or loud, right?! And we should never ask for anything that might appear selfish in a prayer because that's a big no-no. Some even think that prayer won't work unless it's done in a sacred place and you devote a significant amount of time to it (think a multi-hour Sunday Mass). Sitting in traffic is not the right place to blurt out a one-sentence prayer to the divine forces. That couldn't possibly count, could it?

Our goal in this section is to throw a grenade into some of these ideas. We want to reimagine what prayer could look like in our modern lives. And we want to urge you to expand on some of the set-in-stone ideas you might have about this universal, yet deeply individual, conversation with the Source/Universe/Creator.

FIELD NOTES!

Mirror of the Light
by Rainn Wilson

The other day, I was talking to my friend John, who let it slip that he thought that meditation was too hard, but prayer was easy. "I have such ADHD that when I meditate, my mind wanders all over the place like a pachinko ball, but when I'm focused on prayer, I can connect with God in short bursts."

I have another friend, Chris, who meditates every day for at least 20 minutes but finds it *IMPOSSIBLE* to pray. He tells me, "Prayer feels so silly to me. Who am I talking to? A man in the sky? I just can't bring myself to commune with some supernatural force and ask it for help and for things that I want."

This illuminates for me a contemporary American divide, and it's not the political one. Churchgoers often pray without including a meditation practice. And secular folks have no problem meditating but really struggle with the idea of a Higher Power, resisting and recoiling from anything remotely like a prayer.

While the numbers have declined since 2007, the share of Americans who say they pray daily has held at around 45% since 2021. Anecdotally, prayer seems to mostly be undertaken by older adult women and religious conservatives, while meditation is mostly done by young, urban folk.

Prayer is an essential part of all the Abrahamic faiths. Martin Luther once said, "To be a Christian without prayer is no more possible than to be alive without breathing." In Islam, the Quran states, "Oh you who have believed, seek help through patience and prayer." Praying five times a day, the *salat*, is essential to Muslim practice and identity.

Meditation is a fundamental element of the Dharmic religions, such as Hinduism, Jainism, and Buddhism. It is seen as essential toward achieving enlightenment and walking a path of serenity and compassion. In the Western world, it has also become part of the wellness industrial complex—seen as "self-care" that reduces anxiety and maximizes brain effectiveness. Plus, all the apps and classes and corporate coaching have turned meditation into a multi-billion-dollar industry.

Nothing wrong with any of that.

But why the disconnect?

Part of the *Soul Boom* mission is to highlight the importance of engaging in *both* practices. Prayer, to reference Anne Lamott, asks three essential questions of God/Nature/the Cosmic Source: "Help, Thanks, and Wow!" It is beseeching. Striving to commune. Sending a signal up and out from the satellite dish of the human heart.

Meditation is allowing the mind to quiet and that same satellite dish to tune into the deep vibration of the universe by turning inward. To listen for guidance.

In other words, could the two be linked like a transcendent yin and yang walkie-talkie of speaking and listening? Mightn't both be helpful . . . nay, crucial, for balance and spiritual growth?

When our son, Walter, was young, Holiday and I ran a little kids spiritual virtues training class. One of my favorite exercises involved buying a bunch of cheap little mirrors on stands.

"Let's pretend these mirrors are like our hearts!" I would then have the children put them into a coat closet and ask, "Is the mirror reflecting any light?"

"No!" they would chime in. "It's too dark!"

I would then have them take the mirrors outside but point them away from the sun and toward a wall or the ground.

"What about now?"

"No!" they'd all say. "It's pointing in the wrong direction!"

Then (and this was my favorite part), I would bring out buckets of mud and have them cover the mirrors in gunk. "What about now?" Giggles would ensue.

"That's right," I would say. "It's so silly . . . you can't shine the heart with a divine light if it's dirty with gross qualities like greed and anger and meanness, right? You can't shine a light if you stay in the dark. Also, we need to make sure that our little heart-mirrors are pointed at the source of the light if you want to radiate love and joy!"

We would then wash, dry, and polish the mirrors and point them straight at the sun. 'Abdu'l-Baha, the great Baha'i spiritual leader, once said, "Your hearts must be pure and your intentions sincere in order that you may become recipients of the divine bestowals. Consider that although the sun shines equally upon all things, yet in the clear mirror its reflection is most brilliant and not in the black stone."

I would read this quote to the kiddos, and we would quietly reflect on it and the activity for a few minutes before ending the class.

Perhaps we could all learn something from this little children's activity—that prayer AND meditation are needed to keep the satellite dishes/mirrors of our hearts clean, pure, and in a two-way conversation with the light.

> **Marginal Wisdom**
> "I have been driven many times to my knees by the overwhelming conviction that I had absolutely no other place to go."
>
> – Abraham Lincoln, US president

DEFINE

Think about what prayer is to you, and where you believe it comes from. Is it, as many people of faith believe, something that can only come from sacred text or religious figures? Or do you believe any individual can pray, saying anything in their heart? Can atheists "pray"? Who are our prayers to? God? The universe? Where in this spectrum does your perspective lie?

> **Marginal Wisdom**
>
> "Prayer is not asking. It is a longing of the soul. It is a daily admission of one's weakness. It is better in prayer to have a heart without words than words without a heart."
>
> – Mahatma Gandhi, spiritual revolutionary and political activist

EXPLORE

In the last section, we explored meditation and ways to bring more calm, clarity, and reflection into our lives. Does devotion do the same thing? Or does it offer something related but different? What is the difference between prayer and meditation? Novelist Paulo Coelho says, "Prayer is talking with the universe. Meditation is listening to it." Do you think both are important? How do they work together?

> **Marginal Wisdom**
>
> "Prayer may not save us. But prayer may make us worthy of being saved."
>
> – Rabbi Abraham Joshua Heschel, theologian and philosopher

ACTIVITY

WORSHIP WATCH PARTY!

Go to YouTube or TikTok and search for people reciting prayers. Watch a few. Write about your watch party experience below.

What types of prayers from what faith traditions did you experience?

_____
_____
_____
_____
_____

Which prayer gave you "the feels"? What spoke to you about it?

> **Marginal Wisdom**
>
> "The devotees who worship Me with love reside in Me and I reside in them."
>
> – The Bhagavad Gita

_____
_____
_____
_____
_____

How does hearing another person say or chant a prayer affect you differently than reciting it yourself?

_____
_____
_____
_____
_____
_____

Share the link to one of the prayers with a friend. Ask how it made them feel, and record their response here.

_____
_____
_____
_____
_____
_____

★ BONUS ★

Post a video of yourself reciting a prayer! Or send it to us at **submit@soulboom.com**.

EXPLORE

What do you believe is the relationship between prayer and action? Does prayer alone suffice, or is there an element of personal responsibility in what you pray for? Does the idiom "God helps those who help themselves" feel true to you or not? In the Baha'i writings, the great spiritual leader 'Abdu'l-Baha says, "Strive that your actions day by day may be beautiful prayers." Can a prayer BE an action? Can it sometimes be used as an excuse NOT to act? Explore here.

> **Marginal Wisdom**
>
> "Pray as though everything depended on God. Work as though everything depended on you."
>
> – Saint Augustine, Catholic bishop

ACTIVITY

IN SERVICE WE TRUST!

We're going to follow the advice of 'Abdu'l-Baha (see previous page), as well as Jesuit priest Father Michael J. Graham, who once said, "Service is what prayer looks like when it gets up off its knees and walks around in the world."

For one week, do a daily, small act of service in the "spirit of prayer." Clean up a park. Write a note of encouragement and tape it on an elevator button panel. Pay for someone's groceries. You don't need to say a prayer; simply act in the spirit of one. Try not to get any attention or acclaim from your prayerful acts. Journal about it below.

SUNDAY

My act of service:

How it made me feel:

MONDAY

My act of service:

How it made me feel:

TUESDAY

My act of service:

How it made me feel:

WEDNESDAY

My act of service:

How it made me feel:

THURSDAY

My act of service:

How it made me feel:

Marginal Wisdom

"You pray for the hungry. Then you feed them. That's how prayer works."

– Pope Francis

FRIDAY

My act of service:

How it made me feel:

SATURDAY

My act of service:

How it made me feel:

Section 6: The Power of Prayer

ACTIVITY

HELP, THANKS, WOW!

American author Anne Lamott says all prayer boils down to three types: Help, Thanks, Wow. Below, write a personal prayer for each of these three types. We have given you prompts to get you started.

HELP! Think deeply about your biggest challenges or your biggest desires. Now, write a prayer that asks for support and guidance to navigate one of those challenges. Or write a prayer that dares to ask for the thing you want the very most in the world.

My "Help" Prayer: _____

_____

_____

_____

_____

_____

THANKS! What is the absolute best aspect of your life? Is it how connected and happy you are with your family and home life? Your health and the well-being of your loved ones? The love you have for the work you do? Write a prayer of gratitude for the thing that you believe has the most significance in your life.

My "Thanks" Prayer: _____

_____

_____

_____

_____

_____

WOW! Do a Google search for "most beautiful places around me" (because, yes, Google knows where you live). Pick one and drive there. Preferably a place you haven't visited before. Take a walk around the space. When you spy something that makes you pause or a sight that gives you a sense of wonder or awe, pause and say out loud, "Wow." Then, write a prayer from the heart for this moment of bliss.

My "Wow" Prayer: _____

_____

_____

_____

_____

_____

*Now, let's reflect on your three personal prayers.
Did they feel different to you as you were writing them? Which of your three prayers
are you most drawn to saying on repeat right now?*

> **Marginal Wisdom**
>
> "Practice the pause. When in doubt, pause. When angry, pause. When tired, pause. When stressed, pause. And when you pause, pray."
>
> – TobyMac, Christian singer and rapper

REFLECT

There's a saying that suggests God offers three answers to prayers: Yes, No, and Wait. Or even, "Hold on, I've got something better in mind!" Reflect below on your own relationship with prayer within this faith-based context. Some questions to consider:

Have you ever had a prayer that was somehow miraculously answered?

Is the "power of prayer" easier to believe in when the prayers seem to work?

If a prayer doesn't get answered, what does that tell you?

How do you cope when your prayers don't work?

Does prayer make you question (or get angry with) God?

> **Marginal Wisdom**
>
> "Some of God's greatest gifts are unanswered prayers."
>
> – Garth Brooks, country-music singer

DRAW

Prayers that give thanks are one of the most common types, recited by people around the world. Instead of speaking this prayer, we want you to draw a gratitude prayer. Illustrate what you're most grateful for below. It can be a person, a place, or something that is glorious, radiant, or transcendent in your life. Fill it with as much color and light as possible!

> **Marginal Wisdom**
>
> "If the only prayer you ever say in your entire life is thank you, it will be enough."
>
> – Meister Eckhart, Catholic priest and theologian

ACTIVITY

MY PRAYER PRACTICE!

Below is a prayer framework for you to personalize. Fill in the chart below to help you figure out what guidelines and parameters can help you build a prayer practice.

Whom or what will I pray to?
(e.g., God, the universe, my ancestors)

What do I want to pray about?
(e.g., help, gratitude, forgiveness, courage, clarity)

> **Marginal Wisdom**
>
> "I pray every night, sometimes long prayers about a lot of things and a lot of people, but I don't talk about it or brag about it because that's between God and me, and I'm no better than anybody else in God's sight."
>
> – Peyton Manning, football quarterback

Where will I pray?
(e.g., at home, in bed, in church, by my sacred tree, anywhere)

When will I pray?
(e.g., in the morning, daily, whenever I need to)

How will I pray?
(e.g., silently, out loud, in a journal, through dance)

How long will I pray?
(e.g., five minutes, one journal page)

What environment do I want?
(e.g., quiet, scented candles, holding a Bible, it doesn't matter)

Whom will I pray for besides myself?
(e.g., family, community, the planet)

What will remind me it is time to pray?
(e.g., sunrise, an alarm)

How will I know if my prayers are "working"?
(e.g., by how I feel, by my thoughts)

Section 7

VALUES, VIRTUES, *and* MORALITY

IN the classic live-action/animated mash-up film *Who Framed Roger Rabbit*, sexy lounge singer Jessica Rabbit famously says, "I'm not bad. I'm just drawn that way."

It's a brilliant line because, well, she's animated. But it's also an interesting existential question. Are human beings good? Or bad? Are we just drawn that way?

If you ask some Christians, they might say yes, we are born of the "original sin" of Adam and Eve, and it is in our DNA to be "bad." Many atheists also believe that humans are inherently selfish. American psychologist Abraham Maslow wasn't so sure, saying, "Human nature is not nearly as bad as it has been thought to be."

A more nuanced spiritual POV is that human beings—much like Jessica Rabbit—have two natures. One is divine, the other animalistic. Maybe our existential question is simply the internal struggle between these two forces, between conscience and instinct. Why is it that we believe in compassion but complain to an overtaxed waiter when our food is cold? Why do we pray at sunrise and rage-text by lunch?

It's not that our animal nature is "bad." It just wants what it wants when it wants it—food, pleasure, stuff, power, the dopamine rush of doomscrolling. The problem is that modern life demands more of us. It requires us to tap into the parts of us that are patient, kind, graceful. To tap into the "good."

But the question of what exactly is good or bad or right or wrong can be deeply personal and spiritual, informed by culture, faith, upbringing, and life experiences. And this is where our values, virtues, and moral code step into the ring. They help us choose which side of ourselves will win the day—the primal or the divine.

These days, especially in the political arena, politicians, organizers, and ordinary voters adamantly defend their choices, decisions, and policies by saying "I voted my values" or focusing on "issues that matter to me." Which is why we think it's important to devote an entire section of this workbook to exploring your value system, what virtues are important to you, and how you define right and wrong.

Understanding what informs and shapes your personal standards and identifying which ones you prioritize can help you understand your world view and why you make the decisions you do.

It's a universal rubric by which all people make choices. How to be courageous even when it's hard. How to do what you think is right even if it's unpopular. And it's worth digging into.

FIELD NOTES!

Not My Mama's Morality
by Shabnam Mogharabi

"Wait, wait," my mom said, running after my 15-year-old sister, who was about to go on her first date. "Um . . . I wanted to say . . . you know . . . just . . . *no touchy feely*, OK?" She whispered the last part with a concerned *you-understand-me-right?* expression on her face.

My sister stopped short. "Oh my God, Mom. I can't believe you just said that. Yes, OK. This is so embarrassing."

That would be the closest thing to a "sex talk" my parents ever had with us. They're Persian immigrants from a different generation. They imparted life lessons indirectly. My family was loud and joyful, our house was always full of laughter and dancing, and our door was always open to our community. We learned prayers at home, and we went to Sunday school, where we read about virtues like chastity, kindness, courage, and justice. But for the most part, values were modeled in my family, not directly discussed.

My parents never really talked to us about how to navigate the complicated, real-life situations we might find ourselves in as teens or adults. How to deal with peer pressure. What to do when a friend betrays your trust. What a healthy relationship with sex looks like. How to deal with a toxic boss. Conversations like that were not a thing in my family. I learned how to handle those situations via "trial-by-fire" life experiences—which may or may not have been for the best. Who knows?

In fact, in my 20s, I feel like I intentionally rebelled against the family and faith I grew up with. I felt that every idea and principle and value that my parents held close needed to be challenged, rethought, or outright rejected. I had to figure it all out for myself.

These days, as a mom of two young kids, thanks to reading books like *The Whole-Brain Child* and *The Spiritual Child*, as well as being a bit too much of a Dr. Becky Kennedy fan, I approach my parenting differently. I've had age-appropriate conversations with my son about his body. I say things like, "Telling the truth will never, ever make Mommy upset." Or "Wow, this situation feels tricky. Let's brainstorm some ways we can handle it."

I'm hoping that when my kids get older, we can have deeper conversations about what life is really like, all the moral and social quandaries they might face in their futures, and how to make hard choices and decisions. And mostly, that they can feel safe coming to me about anything, so they don't have to figure it all out alone.

But here's the funny thing—while my approach is *very* different, it turns out that the underlying values I hold, the virtues I try to cultivate in them, and the fundamental beliefs I share . . . well, they're largely the same as they were in my childhood. It appears I've come full circle.

A few years back, my sister and I were at my mom's house, talking about some of our old high school friends, when my sister's first date came up. My mom was cracking up at our retelling of her advice antics—she was laughing so hard that we could barely make out every other word, as she said, "Well, it's a good thing you all were such good kids despite me."

We were good kids *because* of you, Mom. And I'm really glad that my foundation of values and beliefs as a mom is based on yours.

> **Marginal Wisdom**
>
> "There's no vocabulary for love within a family, love that's lived in but not looked at, love within the light of which all else is seen, the love within which all other love finds speech. This love is silent."
>
> – T.S. Eliot in *The Elder Statesman*

DEFINE

Below are simple definitions for values, virtues, and morality. Take some time to explore the source of your personal perspective for each of these concepts in your life and your thoughts on how naturally they come to humans.

VALUES. **Values are what you care about and the priorities that matter to you.**
What has influenced and shaped your values in life? Your parents? Church? Country? Why do you think values differ so greatly between people and across cultures?

_____

_____

_____

_____

_____

> **Marginal Wisdom**
>
> "The meaning of good and bad, of better and worse, is simply helping or hurting."
>
> – Ralph Waldo Emerson, poet

_____

_____

_____

_____

_____

_____

_____

_____

_____

_____

_____

_____

_____

_____

_____

_____

_____

_____

_____

_____

VIRTUES. **Virtues are the character traits you exhibit when you're living as your best self.**
Do human beings have an innate sense of what is virtuous? Are virtues divine in nature? Religiously sent? Why do you think so many virtues (like honesty, kindness, courage) are deemed admirable across most every culture, faith, and peoples?

> **Marginal Wisdom**
>
> "To educate a man in mind and not in morals is to educate a menace to society."
>
> – Theodore Roosevelt, US president

MORALITY. **A framework for deciding what is right or wrong; your inner compass.**
Do human beings have an innate sense of what is right or wrong? Do our values and virtues influence our morality? Are your morals, like societal ethics, man-made creations or reflections of some Divine Source?

ACTIVITY

VIRTUES AND VICES!

Let's first spend some time focusing on virtues, those "positive character traits" that most people believe are "good" to cultivate. Below are 100 virtues. Take a minute to read through and study the many qualities outlined here before doing the activity on the next page.

Acceptance	*Creativity*	*Friendliness*	*Mindfulness*	*Righteousness*
Accountability	*Decisiveness*	*Generosity*	*Moderation*	*Sacrifice*
Altruism	*Dedication*	*Gentleness*	*Modesty*	*Serenity*
Appreciation	*Detachment*	*Grace*	*Nobility*	*Service*
Assertiveness	*Determination*	*Gratitude*	*Obedience*	*Simplicity*
Awe	*Devotion*	*Helpfulness*	*Openness*	*Sincerity*
Beauty	*Diligence*	*Honesty*	*Optimism*	*Steadfastness*
Benevolence	*Discernment*	*Honor*	*Orderliness*	*Strength*
Caring	*Discipline*	*Hope*	*Patience*	*Tact*
Certitude	*Empathy*	*Humility*	*Peacefulness*	*Thankfulness*
Cheerfulness	*Endurance*	*Idealism*	*Perceptiveness*	*Thoughtfulness*
Cleanliness	*Enthusiasm*	*Independence*	*Perseverance*	*Tolerance*
Commitment	*Excellence*	*Initiative*	*Playfulness*	*Trust*
Compassion	*Fairness*	*Integrity*	*Prayerfulness*	*Trustworthiness*
Confidence	*Faithfulness*	*Joyfulness*	*Purposefulness*	*Truthfulness*
Consideration	*Fidelity*	*Justice*	*Reliability*	*Understanding*
Contentment	*Flexibility*	*Kindness*	*Resilience*	*Unity*
Cooperation	*Forbearance*	*Love*	*Respect*	*Wisdom*
Courage	*Forgiveness*	*Loyalty*	*Responsibility*	*Wonder*
Courtesy	*Fortitude*	*Mercy*	*Reverence*	*Zeal*

MY TOP 10 VIRTUES

Now consider ... if you had to pick 10 virtues from the ones listed as being the most important to you personally to embody or nurture, which would you pick, and why? Explore below.

	Virtue	Why I value it	How I cultivate it
1			
2			
3			
4			
5			
6			
7			
8			
9			
10			

> **Marginal Wisdom**
>
> "I care. I care a lot. It's kinda my thing."
>
> – Leslie Knope (played by Amy Poehler) in *Parks and Recreation*

MY TOP 10 CHARACTER FLAWS

Looking only at our virtues, without considering our flaws, feels incomplete. In the 12-step program, addicts and alcoholics make a list of their character defects. Not to induce shame but to bring more awareness and consciousness to them and, ultimately, to ask their Higher Power to help release them from these flaws. Let's try a simplified version!

	Flaw	How it shows up	What's required to overcome it
1			
2			
3			
4			
5			
6			
7			
8			
9			
10			

Marginal Wisdom

"I'm responsible for my own happiness? I can't even be responsible for my own breakfast!"

– BoJack Horseman (voiced by Will Arnett) in *BoJack Horseman*

ACTIVITY

VIRTUES OBSERVATION LOG!

Over the next two weeks, look for and seek out virtues in action in the world. It can be a neighbor you know. A stranger at Target. Or someone you read about in the news. Write about what you witnessed, what virtues were at play, why you noticed it, and what you think it reflects about you and your character.

Date & Time: _____
Location: _____
Virtue Witnessed: _____

Reflections: _____
_____
_____
_____
_____

Date & Time: _____
Location: _____
Virtue Witnessed: _____

Reflections: _____
_____
_____
_____
_____

Date & Time: _____
Location: _____
Virtue Witnessed: _____

Reflections: _____
_____
_____
_____
_____

Date & Time: _____
Location: _____
Virtue Witnessed: _____

Reflections: _____
_____
_____
_____
_____

> **Marginal Wisdom**
>
> "When I was a boy and I would see scary things in the news, my mother would say to me, 'Look for the helpers. You will always find people who are helping.'"
>
> – Fred Rogers, minister, author, and children's TV personality

Date & Time: _____
Location: _____
Virtue Witnessed: _____

Reflections: _____
_____
_____
_____
_____

Date & Time: _____
Location: _____
Virtue Witnessed: _____

Reflections: _____
_____
_____
_____
_____

EXPLORE

Beliefs and values are not the same as actions and deeds. In fact, many of us have areas of our lives where there is a disconnect between what we say is important to us and the actions we take. We live in a swirling mass of contradictions. And sometimes, we even live in a way that goes against our values and beliefs. As in, we want world peace, but we cut off cars at a freeway exit (guilty!). Or we are passionate about climate change, but that doesn't stop us from one-click shopping at Amazon or eating red meat (also guilty!).

Write a list of moral contradictions, inconsistencies, or hypocrisies that you live with (and would rather other folks didn't discover about you!).

> **Marginal Wisdom**
>
> "Never let your sense of morals get in the way of doing what's right."
>
> – Isaac Asimov, author

REFLECT

Think of a moment in your life when you had to make a morally complicated or ambiguous decision, one where there was no clear right or wrong answer. Describe the circumstances and what you ultimately chose to do. Are you happy with what you did, or do you regret it? What values guided you? What virtues came in handy? And how did your sense of morality influence what you did—or didn't do?

> **Marginal Wisdom**
>
> "When I let go of what I am, I become what I might be."
>
> – Lao-tzu, ancient philosopher

ACTIVITY

JUDGY MCJUDGERSON!

For many of us, judgment is a constant monologue weighing down our monkey minds, one that is often a reflection of what we value. Make a "judgy mcjudgerson" list by writing down what you judge others for and what you judge yourself for. Let your judge flag fly, so you can cut it loose.

Things I judge others for:

Things I judge myself for:

Looking at your two lists, what do you think this list of judgments tells you about your values? Remember: Don't judge your judgy list. Just observe what it reveals about you.

Marginal Wisdom

"The best attitude to adopt is one of compassionate patience, which has to include a tolerance for failure."

– Gabor Maté, physician and author

ACTIVITY

ALL WHOM I ADMIRE!

Let's now consider the individuals whose moral compass you admire. Below, identify **five** people in your life whom you know, admire, and trust. Focus on those who have an exemplary sense of right and wrong, a high level of integrity, and a deep alignment between their words and actions. Get nitty-gritty about what it is that you most admire about them. Then, craft a compliment that focuses on that.

Who:

My specific compliment:

Who:

My specific compliment:

Who:

My specific compliment:

Who:

My specific compliment:

Who:

My specific compliment:

★ **BONUS** ★

Pick one of the people, pick up the phone, and call them (don't text!). Share your compliment with them.

Marginal Wisdom

"Values are like fingerprints. Nobody's are the same, but you leave them all over everything you do."

– Elvis Presley, rock-and-roll singer

Section 7: Values, Virtues, and Morality

ACTIVITY

MY MAKEUP!

Color in and label the humanoid figure on the next page with the things you value that are of highest priority to you and what percentage of your identity they make up. We've provided an example to help.

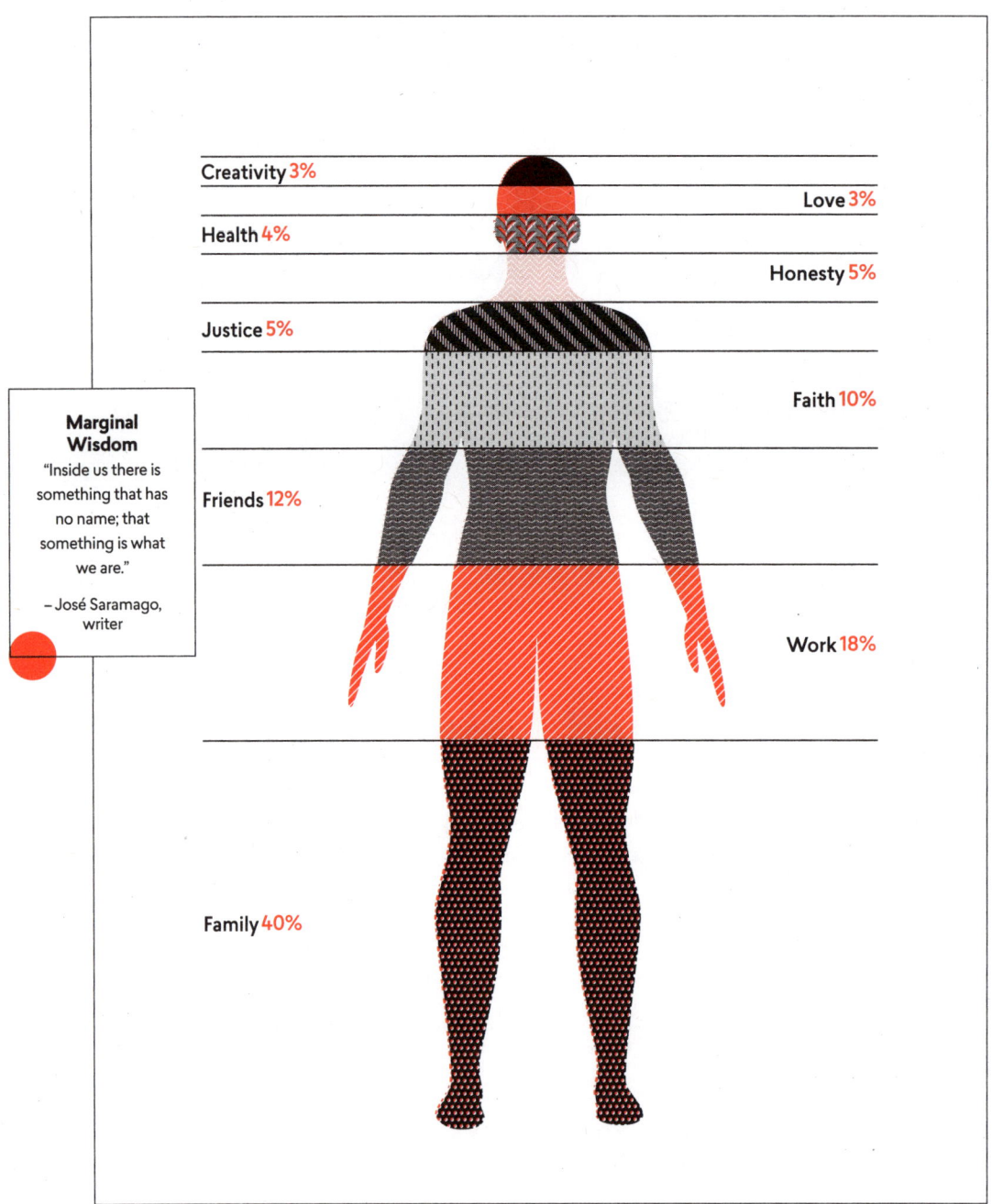

Creativity 3%
Love 3%
Health 4%
Honesty 5%
Justice 5%
Faith 10%
Friends 12%
Work 18%
Family 40%

Marginal Wisdom
"Inside us there is something that has no name; that something is what we are."
— José Saramago, writer

120   Soul Boom Workbook: Spiritual Tools for Modern Living

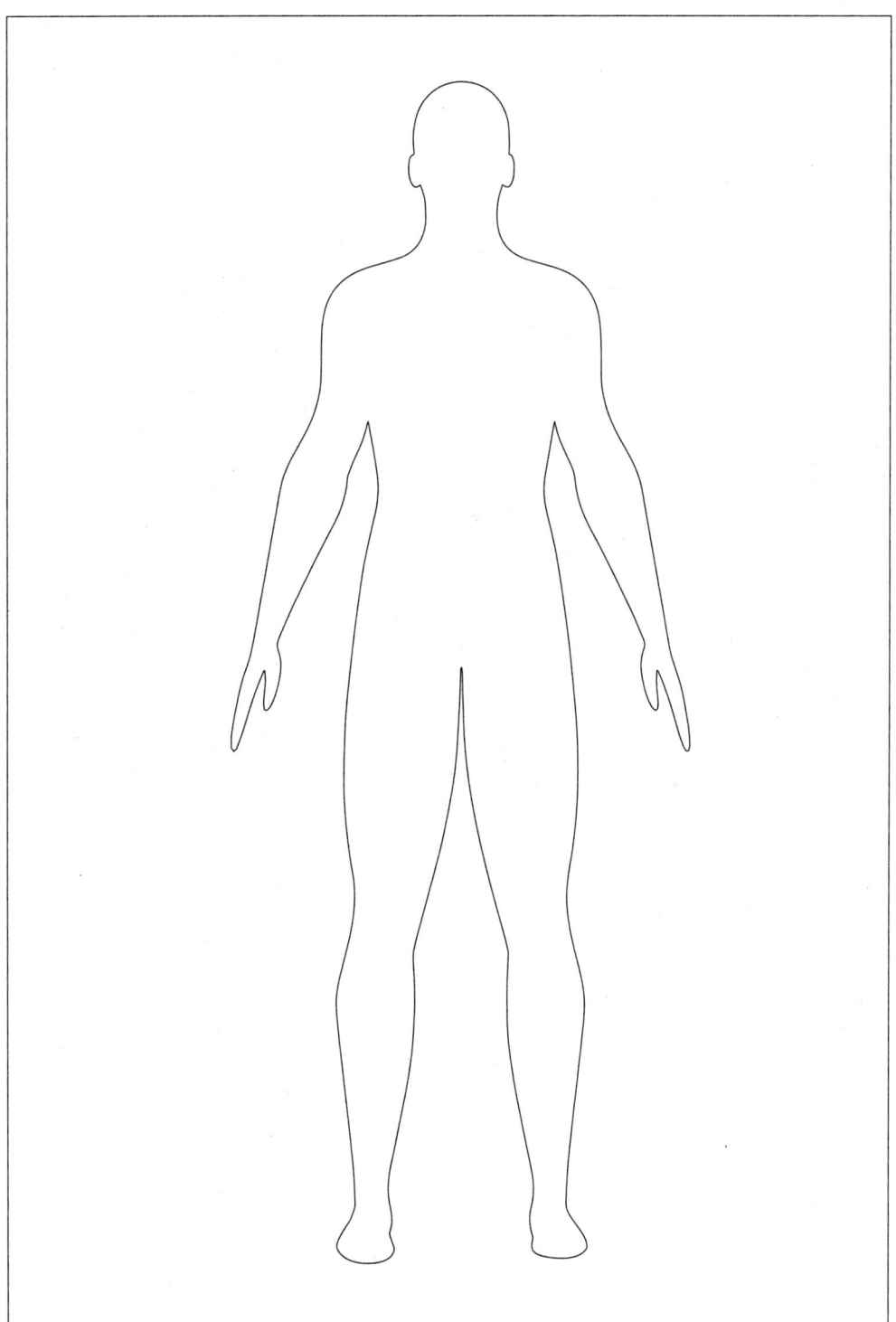

Section 8

BEAUTY, NATURE, and ART

LONG before humanity called it "creation," the world was brimming with creative energy. Trees grew with perfect ring patterns in their trunks. The onslaught of birds chirping in the rainforest was nature's first symphony. The changing colors of the sky were the planet's first fashion show.

This wasn't just the universe being made—it was a work of art. Which raises a pretty profound (if not slightly strange) question: What if all of life were actually born out of an act of creativity? What if the Big Bang were God splashing paint on a multidimensional canvas like Jackson Pollock?

In this section, we're exploring that question. We're exploring creativity as a primal force on the planet. Every time you hear drums in a crashing wave or you stop to admire the way vines curl around your fence, like they know exactly what they're doing, you're engaging with something ancient. Something sacred. Something beautiful.

As poet Dylan Thomas wrote, "The force that through the green fuse drives the flower, drives my green age."

And beauty, nature, and art are how we relate to this creative cosmic force. They remind us that we're not just existing in the universe; we're also an active part of the ongoing masterpiece of its creation.

Nature doesn't create a tree or snowflake because it "needs" to. It creates because that's what it does. It expresses and experiments. It is a maker. And when we humans *make*—when we play or sing, when we admire great art, or when we commune with the mountains or build a sandcastle—then we are participating in that same rhythm.

At *Soul Boom*, we believe that the universe never actually stopped making things—it just started using humans as the vehicle for creation. So as you move through this section, consider that you don't have to be an "artist" to be a creator. You just need to actively engage with all this majestic, swirling creation. To be alive—and maybe a little curious.

FIELD NOTES!

My Uncle, Rhett
by Rainn Wilson

I literally have the most beautiful uncle in the world.

His name is Dr. Rhett Diessner, and no, he's not a model. Not even a beautician. Or a social media influencer. Or even particularly handsome.

He's a specialist in beauty. (And a retired psychology professor.) Specifically, he studied the psychology of beauty and how it affects the ways we see the world, each other, art, nature, and even the choices we make.

Turns out, beauty is a *lot* more important than we think! And, get this, it may be the exact superpower that we humans need to make the world a better place. Because, contrary to contemporary Western society, beauty is not about glamour, makeup, Kardashian fashions, and TikTok hacks. It is also not synonymous with sexual desire.

Plato said, "Beauty is the splendor of truth." It is what is good, harmonious, pleasing, and sublime. In art, nature, and the acts we undertake. And, most importantly, it's something we need to witness and appreciate in other people.

Uncle Rhett says things like this all the time: "One of the most consistent findings of appreciating artistic beauty is that it causes us to be open-minded. In the current political climate, being open-minded is an important cure for stopping the demonizing of political parties we do not belong to. This can help bring about the unity that we need to save the world."

Wait. Beauty is what can save us from toxic partisan politics?!

One of the areas he studies is something I had no idea existed. Moral beauty. Internal beauty. Beauty in action!

Aristotle summed this up as the admiration of the inner qualities of another and how they present in their deeds, as well as your own. Moral beauty is when you or someone you witness performs selfless acts containing virtues, such as kindness, courage, and resilience. Actions that are not done for gain or glory but because of someone's excellence of character. Think Rosa Parks refusing to give up her seat on the bus or a firefighter running into a burning building to save someone.

And what happens when you see and admire someone behaving with moral beauty?

You feel awe. Uplift. And, most importantly, the emotion of *elevation*. Elevation, as named by the great social scientist Jonathan Haidt, is what you feel in your heart when you experience beautiful human action. It elicits a flood of positive hormones like oxytocin that actually prompt one to engage in morally beautiful ways oneself!

That's right. Beauty can call you to action!

Not only that, but having the "beauty appreciation trait," as my uncle calls it, is also a positive indicator of wanting to improve oneself and become a better person. And, according to the data, a love of moral beauty can also predict how much time you take out of your own life to be of service to others.

Similar things happen when you engage with and appreciate artistic or natural beauty. And this is across all cultures in the world!

So perhaps one of the key missing ingredients needed for a spiritual revolution is beauty itself. Educating our children to appreciate and love beauty. Training them (and ourselves) to see beauty in all things. To engage in beautiful actions. To witness the moral beauty of others that propels us to praiseworthy action.

Perhaps beauty is all we need to transform ourselves and our planet!

> **"Beauty will save the world!"**
> **–Fyodor Dostoevsky**
> (and my uncle, Dr. Rhett Diessner)

> **Marginal Wisdom**
>
> "Beauty of whatever kind, in its supreme development, invariably excites the sensitive soul to tears."
>
> – Edgar Allan Poe, poet

DEFINE

WARNING: CREATIVE FREEWRITING AHEAD!

Let's dig into what it truly means to create—not just to make something but to actively participate in the artistic birthing process. Where do you believe creative energy comes from—is it a function of our right brain, an expression of the Source, or something in between? Is creativity a calling or an act of discipline? Are all people inherently creative? Have you ever viewed yourself as not creative, or have you been told you weren't an artist? What do you think has blocked your creativity in the past? We know these are big, meaty questions. So write freely and with abandon.

> **Marginal Wisdom**
>
> "Maybe we are a long way from being made in God's image, but... there has been some progress since then! Such things as art, as poetry, as music... In some kinds of people some tenderer feelings have had some little beginning! That we have got to make grow! And cling to, and hold as our flag! In this dark march toward whatever it is we're approaching..."
>
> – Blanche (played by Vivien Leigh) in *A Streetcar Named Desire*

126 *Soul Boom Workbook: Spiritual Tools for Modern Living*

WRITE

The Navajo have a profound, well-known prayer about beauty:

> *In beauty I walk*
> *With beauty before me I walk*
> *With beauty behind me I walk*
> *With beauty around me I walk*
> *It has become beauty again*

Ancient wisdom tells us that beauty is timeless truths. Beauty calls us to pause, and it stirs something deep inside us. It's mysterious and can transform our hearts. That kind of beauty is not found at a Sephora or New York Fashion Week. In fact, it's getting more difficult to encounter in our daily lives as we rush pell-mell through our commutes, workdays, and family obligations. Yet centering beauty in our steps, our vision, our breath can be crucial to our inner lives.

English playwright Joseph Addison once said, "There is nothing that makes its way more directly to the soul than beauty." Do you long for that kind of soul-moving beauty in your life? How do you define it? Where do you find it most? In your garden? In a crowd of protestors? In the eyes of your children?

Explore your relationship with the great cosmic beauty here.

> **Marginal Wisdom**
>
> "I found I could say things with color and shapes that I couldn't say any other way—things I had no words for."
>
> – Georgia O'Keeffe, painter and artist

Section 8: Beauty, Nature, and Art

ACTIVITY

BEAUTY EMERGENCY!

Inspired by our dear friend Golriz Lucina, we ask you to spend one day making yourself stop, slow down, and enjoy the everyday beauty around you. Take a drive or simply walk through any neighborhood or park. Pay close attention to everything around you, big and small. Every time you see something striking, declare a "Beauty Emergency!" and stop to notice it. An unusual tree. A crack in the sidewalk shaped like a bird. A cyclist in bright neon clothing. Write down all the beauty emergencies that made you stop and pay attention today.

"BEAUTY EMERGENCIES!" SPIED TODAY:

> **Marginal Wisdom**
>
> "Never lose an opportunity of seeing anything beautiful. Beauty is God's handwriting."
>
> – Charles Kingsley, author, professor, and Protestant priest

★ **BONUS** ★

Take a picture of one of your "Beauty Emergency!" moments and send it to someone you love. Tell them why this spoke to you and why you wanted to share it with them. Better yet, start a beauty text group thread!

REFLECT

*Many people struggle with the idea of spirituality but are drawn to experiences of awe and wonder. Atheists don't believe in God but are often drawn to the unimaginable majesty, power, and complexity of the natural world. Think of **five** times in your life when you felt immense wonder or were overwhelmed in amazement. Try to think of at least two that were from your childhood. Where were you? What were you doing? Write about the circumstances and feelings of it.*

1

2

3

4

> **Marginal Wisdom**
>
> "I don't try to imagine a God; it suffices to stand in awe of the structure of the world."
>
> – Albert Einstein, theoretical physicist

5

Section 8: Beauty, Nature, and Art

DRAW

We're willing to bet that at least one of the awe-inspiring moments you wrote about in the previous prompt involved nature. If not, consider the most incredible scene in the natural world you've ever witnessed—the beauty of the Grand Canyon, an encounter with deer in the wild, a constellation of stars in a pitch-black sky.

Now, draw that wonder-filled experience from the natural world below. Like a prayer or reflection of "awe." With color and shape and style, bring to life how the experience stirred your soul.

Marginal Wisdom

"Everybody needs beauty as well as bread, places to play in and pray in, where nature may heal and give strength to body and soul."

– John Muir
in *The Yosemite*

ACTIVITY

STONE STUDY!

*Today, find a small, smooth stone that you like.
Take a walk while holding the stone in your palm.
Every time you notice something beautiful, rub the stone
and express gratitude to it for Earth's beauty.
It's like a pet rock for awesomeness!*

Marginal Wisdom

"The poetry of the earth is never dead."

– John Keats, poet

Section 8: Beauty, Nature, and Art

ACTIVITY

NATURE CONNECT!

Below is a list of elements, plants, and animals in nature that we think merit some attention. Do these with a friend or with a child in your life. Play. Enjoy the bounties of the world around you.

SUN

Go outside on a sunny day. (The "sunny" is important.) Set a timer for 10 minutes. Find the brightest spot that you can and stand there, directly in the sun's warm glow. (Oh, don't forget to put on sunscreen . . . we should have said that first.) Bathe in the warmth. Load up on that natural vitamin D. Extra points if you're barefoot!

GROUND

Connect with the dirt beneath you. Find a garden and stick your fingers in the soil. Feel its life-giving powers. Find a patch of grass and roll around on it. Better yet, find a grassy hill and roll down it!

TREES

For one day, become a literal tree hugger. Go into a grove of trees and start hugging them. Take a walk in your neighborhood and hug every tree you find. (Don't forget your sacred tree. She counts, too.)

WATER

Find a nearby body of water or pond. Stare at its calm, still surface. Wonder about what lies beneath. Now, toss a pebble or rock in. Observe the ripples. Or if you're feeling feisty, splash in, feet first. Let the splashing sounds and spraying droplets remind you of the fluidity of life.

Marginal Wisdom

"The old Lakota was wise. He knew that man's heart away from nature becomes hard; he knew that lack of respect for growing, living things soon led to lack of respect for humans, too."

– Luther Standing Bear, Lakota author

BUGS

dedicated to Shabnam's nephew, Hudson

Lie down on your belly (yes, put those abs to work in a different way) and get at eye level with bugs. Watch an ant commute. Memorize a spider's steady movements. Stare at a roly-poly. Your inner child will be delighted. Your outer adult will survive. Probably.

WIND

Find a breezy spot in your backyard or on a hilltop. Now, talk to the wind. Whisper a secret and let it carry it off. Or share your worries and ask the wind to take one away with it. Feel how it brushes against your skin and tousles your hair.

REFLECT

When asked to talk about a moving piece of art, Rainn once said:

"One of the most transcendent experiences I've ever had was walking down the hallway of the Phillips Gallery in Washington, D.C., and stumbling upon 'Luncheon of the Boating Party' by Renoir. The light poured out of the canvas and filled the space. It was a luminescent snapshot of an afternoon, rich and ripe with humanity—laughter, sweat, and joy. My jaw dropped. It changed the beat of my heart, and I stared at it for a full 15 minutes. I'll never forget that blissful moment."

Now, it's your turn. Write about the most spiritually moving work of art you've ever encountered. We don't care if it's a dance concert, TV show, pop song, or origami. How did the art make you feel? Why do you remember it so potently?

> **Marginal Wisdom**
>
> "In this wonderful new age, art is worship.... That is to say, when thy fingers grasp the paint brush, it is as if thou wert at prayer in the Temple."
>
> – 'Abdu'l-Baha, Baha'i central figure and spiritual leader

Section 8: Beauty, Nature, and Art

ACTIVITY

THE SOUNDTRACK OF MY LIFE

Music has a special power and connection to our memories and pivotal life moments. Build out your personal musical anthology below by completing the chart. Fill in the songs or pieces of music that defined these moments of your life, and why. Do you notice any trends or similarities?

CHILDHOOD

A song someone used to sing to me:	Who sang it, and what do you remember about how they sang it?
The first song (or artist) I ever really loved:	What drew you to it?
The song I associate with family road trips or vacations:	What were your destinations, and who chose the music?

FIRSTS

The song I associate with a school dance or party:	What event, and why?
The song that made me feel seen as a teen:	What were you going through?
The song I associate with my first love:	Which lyrics stood out the most?
The song my friends and I would blast as our anthem:	Who was with you?

Soul Boom Workbook: Spiritual Tools for Modern Living

ADULTING

The song I associate with college:	*What memories does it bring up?*
A song that makes me feel strong when life is tough:	*What have you pushed through?*
The song that hypes me up:	*How does it make you feel?*

LOVE & FAMILY

The song I associate with my partner or wedding:	*Which lyric tells your story?*
The song that helped me through grief or the loss of a loved one:	*Who or what were you mourning?*
A song I sing to someone I love (e.g., a child, a friend):	*Whom do you sing it to, and in what context?*

WHO I AM

The song that reminds me of my culture:	*Where does it take me?*
My guilty pleasure jam:	*What does it remind you of?*
The song that moves me to tears . . . in a beautiful way:	*Which part always gets you?*
The only song I require be played at my funeral:	*What are you telling mourners with this song?*

> **Marginal Wisdom**
>
> "Music is one of the most powerful things the world has to offer. No matter what race, religion, nationality, sexual orientation, or gender that you are, it has the power to unite us."
>
> – Lady Gaga, singer-songwriter and actress

Section 8: Beauty, Nature, and Art

ACTIVITY

DANCE BREAK!

Movement—especially dance—has long been considered a form of sacred spiritual expression. In the Sufi branch of Islam, whirling dervishes spin in meditative circles to get closer to God. King David danced in worship before the Ark in the Bible. Today, people harness the power of dance to create community. Entrepreneur Radha Agrawal (a Soul Boom podcast guest!) does so through her early-morning drug- and alcohol-free Daybreaker dance parties. Movement can clear the mind and open it to new experiences. As dancer Gabrielle Roth said, "The fastest way to still the mind is to move the body."

In fact, a 2024 Australian study looked at various forms of movement and exercise and the effect they had on treating depression compared to standard SSRIs (antidepressant medication). Universally, exercise was good for our mental health. (Duh!) Most forms of cardio outranked drugs in creating better outcomes for depression. But as neuroscientist and author Erik Hoel pointed out, the highlight of the study was this: Just dancing has the best outcome of ANY other treatment, exercise, or drug for depression.

What a wild and beautiful and oh-so-human truth. Dance is one of the most powerful forms of movement there is for our mental health—and also for spiritual expression. So, as James Brown once said, "Get up off that thing. Dance, and you'll feel better."

Marginal Wisdom

"To dance is to be out of yourself. Larger, more beautiful, more powerful."

– Agnes de Mille, ballet dancer and choreographer

ASSIGNMENT

Put on the most soulful (and soul-stirring) song you can and dance to it with wild abandon. Let your heart and spirit guide your movement. Don't worry, no one is watching!

ACTIVITY

BE A FASHIONER!

In Islam, one of the names of God is Al-Musawwir, or "the Fashioner," because he's believed to have created the universe out of nothing. Humans have long seen a blank page or an empty stage and filled it with explosions of artistry. In emulation of the Fashioner, George R. R. Martin, J. K. Rowling, and J. R. R. Tolkien built entire worlds that didn't exist before. Now is your turn to channel a Big Bang moment of creativity. Here are a few blank pages. Each page is an opportunity to imagine, draw, write, and "fashion" something that did not exist before.

Marginal Wisdom

"The purpose of art is washing the dust of daily life off our souls."

– Pablo Picasso, painter

PAUSE & PONDER

Congratulations! You're halfway through your personal spiritual journey!

In this second unit, we sought to unfurl and help you better understand the many layers that make up your inner spiritual life. We defined and played with the ideas of what is sacred and of meditation and prayer; we defined the values and virtues that shape the moral compass; and we explored what it's like to commune with all creation.

Take a minute to flip back through the pages of Part Two. Reflect on your journey thus far below.

What was your favorite writing prompt, reflection, or activity? Why? What did it reveal about yourself?

Which prompt, reflection, or activity was the most challenging for you or made you the most uncomfortable? Why do you think that is?

As you head into the next part, which explores how spirituality can help us deal with the messy parts of being human, what are your biggest takeaways from this unit of work?

Draw, doodle, or sketch any final images that pop into your head as you move forward on your spiritual journey.

USE THIS SPACE TO CONTINUE EXPLORING!

Part
THREE

Digging Deep

In Which We Wrestle with the Hard Stuff

Section 9:
Anxiety and Mental Health

Section 10:
Tests and Difficulties

Section 12:
The Meaning of Life

Section 11:
Death and Dying

Hey there.

Part Three deals with some tough, messy, and triggering subjects. It's going to get a little dark and difficult for the next several pages.

The first three sections of this block of work tackle anxiety, depression, and mental health; the suffering we experience from life's tests and difficulties; and the topic of death and dying.

If you are at a point in your life where exploring these subjects is too hard—and you're just not feeling it—we totally get it. Feel free to skip ahead to Section 12, which digs into something much more elevating and potentially inspiring—the meaning of life!

Be kind to yourself. Take your time.
You can always come back to the hard stuff later.

With love and compassion,
Rainn and Shabnam

Section 9

ANXIETY
and
MENTAL HEALTH

INT. A COZY BEDROOM - NIGHT

SOUND of a steady, deep snore. There is a DIM GLOW coming from a night light. ANNA (30s) lies in bed. She's tossing and turning. Her husband, MARK (30s), is passed out next to her…the snoring is coming from him. She stares at him, annoyed, then punches him. The snoring stops…and starts again 10 seconds later. She sighs and looks up at the ceiling.

ANNA (INTERNAL MONOLOGUE)
Why did I say "you too" when the waiter told me to enjoy my meal? If I drink more water now, will I have to pee at 4 a.m.? Should I be concerned that our creepy neighbor's Wi-Fi is called "QAnon4Evah!"? If I had a cell phone in medieval times, would they think I'm a witch? I need to declutter the silverware drawer tomorrow…we can't keep using the same two forks. If I fall asleep now, I'll get exactly 5 hours and 7 minutes of sleep. Which is probably fine…right? Or is it? I have to pee. Again.

THIS scene feels like it could be someone you know, right? It's pretty . . . *human.*

Our brains love to do this. Overthink. Spiral. Distract. Consider all the things that don't really matter while avoiding the big, juicy questions like . . . Who is most important to me? Does my work fulfill me? What am I going to do with this one wild, precious life?

This third unit of the *Soul Boom Workbook* is all about the hard, messy stuff of being a human. Because spirituality is not just meditation in poppy fields with loving friends. Spirituality matters most when things get hard. And this section kicks off with one of the most challenging struggles that lives inside us—the over-stimulated, overthinking, deceptively tricky noisiness of our minds.

The most common mental health disorder in our interconnected world is anxiety. In 2019, 301 million people worldwide were clinically diagnosed as suffering from it, according to the World Health Organization (WHO). Undiagnosed cases run much higher, of course.

For most of human history, anxiety was a good thing! Warning us of impending danger and keeping us alert. But the world has changed significantly since the Industrial Revolution. Now, with distractions and dangers everywhere, we're overwhelmingly on a constant high alert.

And this neural overload is happening all over the world in all sorts of ways:

- In the United States, 29% of adults have been diagnosed with depression at some point in their lives, according to Gallup News. And that number has increased nearly 10 percentage points from 2015 to now.
- WHO declared loneliness a "global public health concern" in 2023, reporting that 23% of adults worldwide feel lonely "a lot of the day." That means more than one out of five adults on the planet experience significant loneliness. (Plus, the increased risk of premature death from loneliness is equivalent to smoking 15 cigarettes a day.)
- Loneliness has increased precipitously for younger generations. A 2020 Cigna study found that 79% of adults ages 18 to 24 feel lonely every day or multiple times a week, compared to 41% of seniors ages 66 and older.
- In 2023, one person died by suicide every 11 minutes in the United States, according to the Centers for Disease Control and Prevention. And globally, WHO reports that suicide accounts for one out of every 100 deaths, making it the third-leading cause of mortality among individuals ages 15 to 29.

The truth is that there are powerful ways to cope with all of these growing concerns that aren't found on a doctor's prescription pad. At *Soul Boom*, we take a page from Tibetan Buddhists and start with compassion as one of many tools to reduce suffering. Not just in the form of empathy but also as a commitment to action to make life better for others.

We will tackle this and other solutions to the challenges of the mind with a heavy focus on anxiety, which can often lead to so many other isolating tendencies. We want to help you understand how and when it shows up in your life. We'll help you identify your triggers and calm your mind. And we will, hopefully, support you in designing a plan for mental well-being.

This stuff is hard. So let's be kind, compassionate, and spiritually grounded as we dig in. And let's decide how we want to rewrite the "movie scene" monologue playing in our anxious minds.

END SCENE

FIELD NOTES!

Mr. Anxiety

by Rainn Wilson

I'm looking intently at an empty chair across from me in a cluttered, poorly furnished room, and I say, "I see you. I know what you're doing. And you know what? All I want to do is give you a hug."

From the outside, I might look like an imbalanced nutjob, talking to an imaginary friend, but there's a method to this particular madness.

An old elf of a man sits on the other side of the room and is watching the proceedings with a kind of compassionate laser vision. This is Bruce. My therapist.

"Good. Keep going. Tell it what you need," he says.

"I know you want what's best for me. I know you're there to protect me. You're looking out for me. But what you really need is a hug," I say. "What *I* really need is a hug. That's what I need most of all."

And I literally begin to hug myself, drinking in the feeling of my arms around myself. Right there in this dusty therapist's office above a parking lot in Van Nuys, California.

Embarrassing to admit, but there you are.

You see, what I'm doing is having a conversation with my anxiety. Pretending that it is literally sitting in that empty chair across from me. And when I'm done with what I have to say, I switch. I go sit in that chair, take on the role of Mr. Anxiety, and talk to the empty one I was just sitting in.

The character I always dreamed of playing—Rainn Wilson's anxiety—now talking to me, Rainn Wilson.

Apparently, this "chair work" exercise is from Gestalt therapy. It may seem and sound ridiculous. But damn if it doesn't work. Over time.

You see, there's a chorus of forces at work in our heads. It's like there's a boardroom of voices inside us that have lots to say. Sometimes at the most inopportune times. It's like the movie *Inside Out* coming to life. But with a heavy dose of Sigmund Freud and Carl Jung.

Here are some of the possible personality archetypes that might jab at you occasionally from inside the old cranium. Ones you might initiate a Gestalt "chair work" dialogue with:

- The critical father's voice
- The fearful voice of your inner child
- The "less than" voice
- The resistance that holds you back
- The rebellious teenager
- Your addictions
- Your phobias
- Your self-sabotaging nature

Depending on what you're going through, you initiate back-and-forth dialogue, portraying, at one point, your most wise/cogent self, and at others, that internal disruptive force responding back.

So much gets uncovered. Peeled back. Illumined.

On this specific day, I'm slowly revealing the reality that my anxiety is actually looking out for me! It's trying to alert me. Protect me. From what? The unknown. The possibility of pain.

Mr. Anxiety is just a little too dominant most of the time. Not right-sized. Overwhelming.

And, as Bruce always tells me, your anxiety is a red flag. It's a helpful warning. But let it guide you toward what you *truly* need. Deep down. In your body. In your heart.

The antidote for Mr. Anxiety's too-strong voice? It's to, first off, greet my anxiety by acknowledging it: "Hi there, Mr. Anxiety. I see you churning and warning and poking. I witness you."

And then I go to the next level: "And what do I really need, Mr. Anxiety? A hug. Soothing. A reminder that so much is out of my control, and I am now giving that over to God and the universe. And today, I will only address what is actually *IN* my control."

At the end of the day, it's the "Serenity Prayer" that provides the best path forward to deal with my new friend Mr. Anxiety and his chorus of cohorts in my head:

> *"God, grant me the serenity to*
> *accept the things I cannot change,*
> *the courage to change the things I can,*
> *and the wisdom to know the difference."*

And all you need is two chairs!

Marginal Wisdom

"To realize that you are not your thoughts is when you begin to awaken spiritually."

– Eckhart Tolle, author and philosopher

REFLECT

Anxiety, stress, worry, and loneliness can be warning flags trying to alert you to a deeper need. Let's explore what anxiety or worry looks like in your life. What could it be trying to tell you? What might it be signaling to you? What needs might your loneliness or depression want you to fulfill?

> **Marginal Wisdom**
>
> "Anxiety's like a rocking chair. It gives you something to do, but it doesn't get you very far."
>
> – Jodi Picoult, writer

EXPLORE

Given how prevalent anxiety is in the world, we want to give you a chance to explore your own relationship with it. Maybe you're a high-anxiety person; maybe anxiety shows up only rarely in your life. Wherever you lie on the spectrum, understanding when and where your anxiety is triggered can be a useful exercise and a powerful tool for managing stressful situations. Give it a try.

I feel most anxious when: _____

Marginal Wisdom

"Leave your front door and your back door open. Allow your thoughts to come and go. Just don't serve them tea."

– Shunryu Suzuki, author and Zen monk

If my anxiety is triggered, I tend to emotionally feel: _____

My body physically reacts by: _____

My behavior changes in that I am likely to: _____

I know my anxiety is trying to keep me safe by telling me: _____

_____

_____

_____

_____

_____

Some of the things that help my mind and body in moments of anxiety are:

- ☐ Taking a deep breath
- ☐ Going for a short walk
- ☐ Yoga or stretching
- ☐ Exercising or breaking a sweat
- ☐ Taking a bath or shower
- ☐ Doing something creative
- ☐ Writing or journaling
- ☐ Making a to-do list
- ☐ Turning off the news
- ☐ Taking a social media break
- ☐ Spending time in nature
- ☐ Sleeping or taking a nap
- ☐ Listening to music
- ☐ Watching a favorite show or film
- ☐ Seeking out laughter
- ☐ Eating a healthy snack
- ☐ Reducing coffee, alcohol, or sugar
- ☐ Using CBD oil
- ☐ Drinking hot water or tea
- ☐ Taking a cold plunge
- ☐ Talking to a loved one or friend
- ☐ Hugging someone
- ☐ Hugging yourself
- ☐ Snuggling with a dog or cat
- ☐ Seeing my therapist
- ☐ Other: _____
- ☐ Other: _____

In general, I am best able to let go of or process my anxiety by: _____

_____

_____

_____

_____

_____

_____

No matter what, I can love my anxiety as part of me. In fact, next time I experience anxiety, I will fill out this statement and repeat it **five** times:

Thank you, Anxiety, for warning me about: _____

I know you are trying to keep me safe from: _____

Anxiety, you are not me. And I can accept your message without being defined by it.

Section 9: Anxiety and Mental Health

ACTIVITY

ALWAYS BE REFRAMING!

The Baha'i writings say, "The reality of man is his thought." And the Buddha famously said, "We are what we think. All that we are arises with our thoughts. With our thoughts, we make the world." So how do we cultivate good thoughts, especially when we have evolved to have a negative tendency built into our brains? By reframing, of course!

One simple way to do this is to eliminate the words "have to" or "don't want to" from our inner monologue and vocabulary. Replacing them with "I get to" or "I choose to" flips our inner thoughts upside down—and instills gratitude and affirmation.

*So let's start! Write down **five** thoughts you have had recently that could use a good reframe. Then, flip each thought on its head! Write a new reality! Ready? Go!*

Example. My thought: I have to go to work. **My reframe:** I get to go to work.

My thought: _____

My reframe: _____

My thought: _____

My reframe: _____

> **Marginal Wisdom**
>
> "For him who has conquered the mind, the mind is the best of friends."
>
> – The Bhagavad Gita

My thought: _____

My reframe: _____

My thought: _____

My reframe: _____

My thought: _____

My reframe: _____

ACTIVITY

MY SPIRITUAL TOOL KIT!

We just explored ways to soothe or support your mind and body through anxiety—whether that's reframing your thoughts, taking a hot shower, or snuggling your pet pig (or maybe that's just Rainn). Now, we want you to consider spiritual solutions to anxiety. Below is a basic spiritual tool kit for anxiety management. Give these tactics a try.

TOOL #1: Do a *Metta* Meditation.

In Buddhism, a *metta* meditation focuses on loving-kindness toward yourself and others as a way to cultivate compassion and a strong sense of connection with others. Fill in some metta meditations below. (We've given you some examples to start.) Now, find your favorite meditating spot and begin repeating them. Feel love echo for yourself and those around you.

Examples:

May I be kind and gentle with myself. May you be kind and gentle with yourself.

May I be healthy in mind and body. May you be healthy in mind and body.

May I be _____ May you be _____
_____ _____

May I be _____ May you be _____
_____ _____

May I be _____ May you be _____
_____ _____

May I be _____ May you be _____
_____ _____

May I be _____ May you be _____
_____ _____

May I be _____ May you be _____
_____ _____

TOOL #2: Pray to God.

Write a prayer asking God to take away your difficulties, pain, anxiety, or mental suffering. If you have a hard time thinking of one, we've included one of our favorites for difficult times. Say the prayer as many times as you need to feel that the all-embracing Source of Universal Love has heard it and to feel a sense of surrender to a power greater than yourself.

A Baha'i prayer:
> *"Is there any Remover of difficulties, save God? Say: Praised be God!*
> *He is God! All are His servants, and all abide by His bidding!"*

Your prayer to God (make one up or pull from your faith tradition):

_____
_____
_____
_____
_____
_____
_____
_____

TOOL #3: Seek Out Worship.

Sometimes, stepping into a spiritual or religious space and engaging in worship with others can be profoundly soothing. Find a place of worship near you and join in, even if you sit quietly in the back. Enjoy watching your human family pray and worship with something greater. Can't think of where to go? Below are some suggestions.

- Offer flowers and burn incense with others at a Hindu temple.
- Attend Friday prayers at a local mosque.
- Enjoy the structure of Sunday Mass at a Catholic church.
- Join a Shabbat service in a synagogue.
- Attend a seasonal or pagan nature ceremony.
- Go to a Baha'i musical devotional gathering.
- Listen to a gospel music performance at a church.
- Participate in readings at a Unitarian Universalist fellowship night.
- Sit in silence at a Quaker meeting house.

TOOL #4: Listen to Spiritually Inspired Music.

We know this might mess up your perfectly curated Spotify Wrapped, but it's worth it! We promise! Ask Google or ChatGPT to recommend some spiritual artists in a group, religion, or genre that interests you. Listen to a few songs. Immerse yourself in the sound of words inspired by spiritual themes, even when you don't understand the lyrics or language. Focus on the music, not on your mind. If you don't know where to start, we've curated a possible list below.

Enya *Celtic spiritual singer*	**Sufjan Stevens** *spiritual singer*	**Matisyahu** *Jewish rapper*
Luke Slott *Baha'i singer-songwriter*	**Mordechai Shapiro** *Jewish singer*	**Indian Ocean** *Hindu musical group*
Maher Zain *Muslim artist*	**Switchfoot** *Christian alt rock*	**Karim Rushdy** *Baha'i rapper*
CeCe Winans *Gospel singer*	**Elisapie** *Indigenous (Inuk) musician*	**Tibetan Singing Bells Monks** *Buddhist musicians*
Kanhiya Mittal *Buddhist Indian artist*	**Lauren Daigle** *Christian artist*	**Skillet** *Christian hard rock band*
Sigur Rós *Spiritual rock band*	**Imee Ooi** *Buddhist chanter*	**Alex Boyé** *Mormon singer*

TOOL #5: Commune with Nature.

Native and Indigenous peoples have long believed that nature's rhythms can provide peace, calm, and harmony to our spirits. Seek out a place in nature and find its rhythm—the kind that feels grounding, meditative, even musical. Think the sound of waves crashing on a shore, a chorus of crickets chirping at night, the pops of a crackling fire, or the sound of leaves rustling in the wind. Close your eyes and breathe in sync with the elements around you. Feel how these sounds of nature not only soothe but also connect you to some larger peace and meaning.

> **Marginal Wisdom**
>
> "You can worry, or you can worship. You can't do both. Choose wisely."
>
> – Rick Warren, Christian evangelical pastor

ACTIVITY

BREATHE IT OUT!

Here's a fascinating factoid: How we breathe shapes how we feel. If you've ever taken a yoga class, you know that breathing is a big part of the "flow" state. Science also tells us that breathing is a superpower—it activates our parasympathetic nervous system (our "rest and digest" mode) to reduce our heart rate and blood pressure. In fact, a Harvard study found that taking six deep breaths per minute can reduce stress hormones and promote calm. Since breathing is usually automatic, controlled breath work actually sends signals to our brain that we're safe.

Now, it's time to whip out this secret weapon for your own well-being. Find a quiet place and consider something you're anxious or nervous about. Set a timer for five minutes. Reflect on this thought while doing one of the following breathing techniques.

OPTION 1

Box breathing is a technique popularized by Mark Divine, a former Navy SEAL. It helps to visualize a box and to remember that each inhale, hold, exhale, hold moment lasts four seconds. If you've never tried **4-4-4-4** box breathing, we have a handy visual for you.

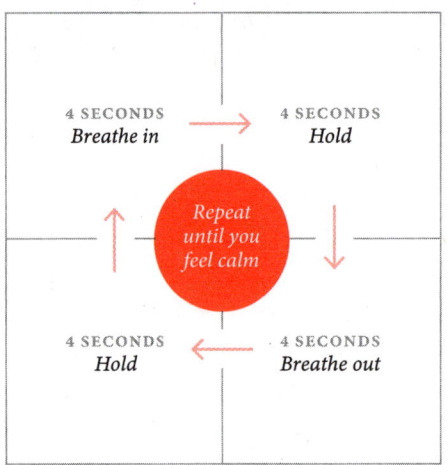

OPTION 2

Dr. Andrew Weil, an integrative medicine practitioner, developed the **4-7-8** breathing technique. You inhale for four seconds, hold for seven seconds, and exhale for eight seconds. One of the critical parts of this practice is to make a strong "whoosh" sound as you blow out.

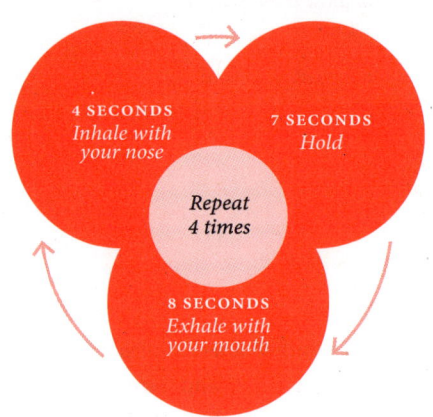

Marginal Wisdom

"Feelings come and go like clouds in a windy sky. Conscious breathing is my anchor."

– Thich Nhat Hanh, Buddhist monk and peace activist

How did this exercise make you feel?

_____
_____
_____
_____
_____

ACTIVITY

TIME FOR A WEEKLY WORRY!

And now an idea courtesy of Dr. Jill Gaoghagan, Shabnam's kids' pediatrician! Create a "Weekly Worry Window" appointment in your calendar. Set aside a 20-minute window once a week. Then, as news headlines, setbacks, and other stressors arise, do not dwell on them. Simply write them down in a journal, put them in the Notes app on your phone, or add them to the calendar invite. Tell yourself, "I'll worry about that later."

Then, do not worry about it any longer. In fact, worry less and remind yourself it's not time yet! When your "Weekly Worry Window" appointment arrives, pull out your list and read through it. Which things are you still worried about? Which did you let go of as you created space between the worry and your reaction to it? Which do you want to take time to think about or research before reacting to?

Marginal Wisdom

"Worrying means you suffer twice."

– Newt Scamander (played by Eddie Redmayne) in *Fantastic Beasts and Where to Find Them*

ACTIVITY

SERENITY COLORING PAGE!

The serenity prayer is a short, powerful prayer commonly attributed to theologian Reinhold Niebuhr. Below, this prayer has been designed into beautiful, intricately decorated word art for you to color in. Why? During the COVID-19 pandemic, coloring books, especially those with detailed images, became all the rage. The reason is that the soothing, relaxing activity of meticulously coloring a page helps us stay present and grounded, according to the Art Therapy Project, a New York nonprofit. So grab your colored pencils and get to work. Focus on every stroke, shade, and detail. Notice how your body feels as you slowly fill in every inch.

ACTIVITY

THE YIN-YANG OF SERENITY

Now, let's put the serenity prayer you meditatively colored on the previous page into action. Below is a blank Yin-Yang diagram. One side is labeled "Out of my control," and the other is labeled "Within my control." Start listicling! Think about all the things currently creating stress or anxiety in your life. For each item that you list as being out of your control, simply write the words "thank you" or "I will pray about this" next to them. For every item that you list as being within your control, write a small, simple action that you can take to address it.

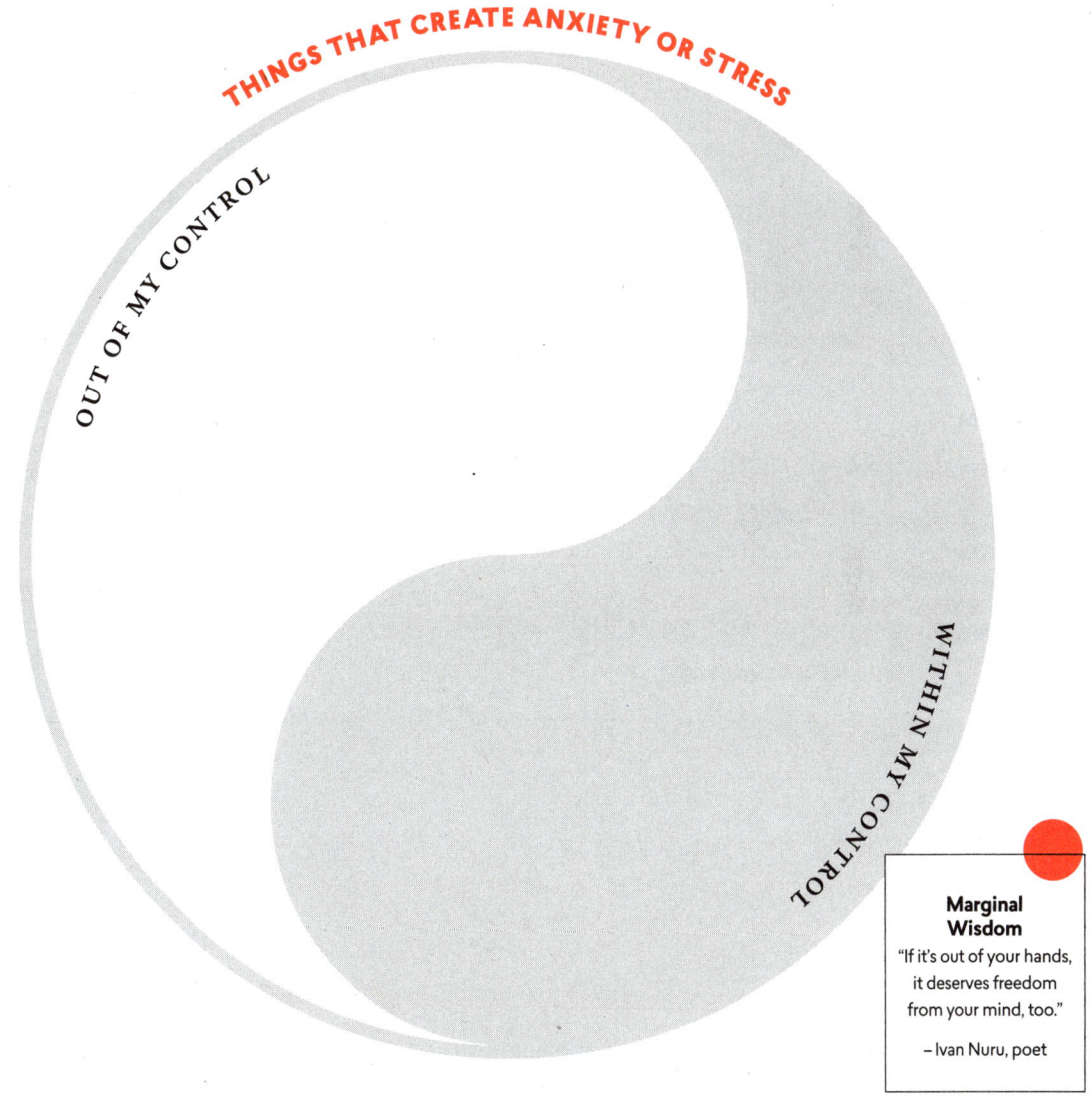

THINGS THAT CREATE ANXIETY OR STRESS

OUT OF MY CONTROL

WITHIN MY CONTROL

Marginal Wisdom

"If it's out of your hands, it deserves freedom from your mind, too."

— Ivan Nuru, poet

ACTIVITY

ME, MYSELF, AND MY ANXIETY!

The brilliant Brené Brown, a psychologist, author, and expert on shame and vulnerability, often says, "Talk to yourself like you would to someone you love." We are going to practice that skill now. Below, we want you to think about all the ways that your mental health has affected your life. Write a conversation between your troubled mind and your loving self. Think of responding to a thought like "You really screwed up today" with a loving "I forgive you, and you'll get another chance." Practice embracing your mind with all the love and compassion you can channel.

I struggle with:

- ☐ Anxiety
- ☐ Loneliness
- ☐ Social isolation
- ☐ Depression

- ☐ Anger management
- ☐ Panic attacks
- ☐ Addiction
- ☐ Screen dependence

- ☐ Other: _____
- ☐ Other: _____
- ☐ Other: _____
- ☐ Other: _____

> **Marginal Wisdom**
>
> "We can still be crazy after all these years. We can still be angry after all these years. We can still be timid or jealous or full of feelings of unworthiness. The point is not... to try to throw ourselves away and become something better. It's about befriending who we are already."
>
> – Pema Chodron, Tibetan Buddhist nun

Me (Troubled Mind):
_____

Me (Loving Self):
_____

Me (Troubled Mind):
_____

Me (Loving Self):
_____

Me (Troubled Mind):
_____

Me (Loving Self):
_____

Me (Troubled Mind):
_____

Me (Loving Self):
_____

Me (Troubled Mind):
_____

Me (Loving Self):
_____

ACTIVITY

STAY IN THE NOW!

Buddhists know that presence is often the antidote to anxiety, worry, panic attacks, and other mental health challenges. Being aware of your body, breath, and surroundings in a single moment can often keep the mental loops caused by time travel (regret about the past and worries about the future) at bay.

Eckhart Tolle, the self-help author whose book The Power of Now *expands deeply on this single idea, says, "You are not your mind; you are the awareness behind it." Try this simple meditation to test this approach out for yourself. Find a quiet, comfortable place. As you slowly breathe in and out, read and reflect on the words below.*

BREATHE.
THERE IS ONLY NOW.
The past is gone. Dwelling on it will not help. Let the past go.
The future doesn't exist. It is an illusion.
There is only now.

BREATHE.
THERE IS ONLY NOW.
Let every breath bring you back to the present moment.
Notice the softness of your breath as it comes into your nostrils and out your lips.
Let the thoughts that ping around your mind like popcorn float away.
There is only now.

BREATHE.
THERE IS ONLY NOW.
Listen to the sounds around you, the distant ones, the near ones.
Listen for the silence of the space between the sounds.
There is only now.

BREATHE.
THERE IS ONLY NOW.
You are not your thoughts.
You are not your feelings.
You are not your ego.
You are stillness.
You are presence itself.
Just be in the now.

BREATHE.

Marginal Wisdom

"Peace is the result of retraining your mind to process life as it is, rather than as you think it should be."

– Dr. Wayne Dyer, self-help author and motivational speaker

ACTIVITY

LEARN A "GRANDMA HOBBY"!

We've given you a lot of ways to internally manage and respond to anxiety. Now, it's time for something to do! Time to LEARN! Learning is exceptionally good for our mental well-being. A 2018 study in the journal Psychological Medicine *found that people who participated in a six-week leisure activity, such as learning music or taking a creative writing class, without any "goal" at the end, reported significant reductions in anxiety and depression symptoms and a stronger sense of purpose. And learning requires curiosity, a critical quality to cultivate on any spiritual journey!*

Unfortunately, as adults, we stop learning solely for the joy of learning. We often internalize thoughts like "I didn't pick that up right away, I must not be good at it." Or "I fell again. This is embarrassing. I'm going to stop." We only work to acquire new skills (especially those outside our comfort zones) to get ahead at work, win a prize, or get a gold star. Yet pure learning can be a true antidote to anxiety, stress, and depression.

Interestingly, learning one type of activity in particular—slow-paced, old-fashioned ones— has some bonus benefits! A 2025 study in the British Journal of Occupational Therapy *found that individuals who engaged in knitting or sewing reported feeling calmer, less stressed, and more uplifted. It's no wonder* The Wall Street Journal *reported shortly thereafter that these types of activities are on the rise with 20-somethings. So let's give it a try!*

Below is a list of 21 "grandma (and grandpa) hobbies"—old-fashioned and surprisingly soothing for our mental health. Read through and pick **one** *that is appealing—one that you're not already good at!*

☐ Knitting or crocheting
☐ Embroidery
☐ Whittling or woodworking
☐ Quilting
☐ Beekeeping
☐ Scrapbooking
☐ Calligraphy

☐ Ceramics or pottery
☐ Origami
☐ Coin or stamp collecting
☐ Baking bread
☐ Canning
☐ Flower arranging
☐ Gardening

☐ Handwriting letters
☐ Slow smoking meats
☐ Genealogy research
☐ Birdwatching
☐ Fishing
☐ Candle making
☐ Rock tumbling

Now comes the hard part. Sign up for a class, watch some YouTube tutorials, and see what happens! Don't worry about improving—just be present with your curiosity, hands, and the motions of the work. After a few sessions, reflect on what it feels like to learn something, slow and steady, without an endgame.

> **Marginal Wisdom**
>
> "The more that you read, the more things you will know. The more that you learn, the more places you'll go."
>
> – Dr. Seuss
> in *I Can Read with My Eyes Shut!*

Section 10

TESTS
and
DIFFICULTIES

ONE of the oldest and most important spiritual/philosophical conversations is around the question: How can there be an all-loving God when there is so much suffering in the world?

Sure, if we had it our way, life would be hanging out on a sailboat at sunset, eating burrata and fig jam crostini while Beatles albums play in the background. But instead, life is often made up of traffic jams, awkward conversations, canceled flights, gaining weight, getting fired, financial stress, breakups and breakdowns, the diagnosis of illness, and the funerals that follow.

Yet in nearly every spiritual practice in the world—from Buddhist monks to grandmas praying in church on Sunday—there's a radical idea that keeps coming up: *THE MESS MATTERS.*

It's a bold hypothetical question to ponder: What if *suffering* was what this world was all about? Author Elizabeth Gilbert calls our one precious life "Earth School." The wounds of our lives are not problems for us to fix but openings that can teach, stretch, and even transform us ... if we let them.

Leonard Cohen wrote in the song "Anthem":

There is a crack, a crack in everything
That's how the light gets in

What a beautiful and life-altering idea: What is broken is what allows the light of transformation in. It reminds us of this beautiful passage from a letter written by the wise Baha'i spiritual leader 'Abdu'l-Baha to someone suffering:

"The more difficulties one sees in the world, the more perfect one becomes. The more you plough and dig the ground, the more fertile it becomes. The more you cut the branches of a tree, the higher and stronger it grows. The more you put the gold in the fire, the purer it becomes.... Therefore, I am happy that you have had great tribulations and difficulties. Strange it is that I love you and still I am happy that you have sorrows."

At *Soul Boom*, we believe true spirituality gets in the muck with us in difficult times. It sits with our grief. It listens to our anxieties. It holds space for the mystery of not knowing why something happened in our lives ... and gives us the strength to walk forward anyway.

If you've ever been to therapy, you know that naming your pain, being present with it, and finding meaning within it is all part of healing. In fact, Buddhist monk and peace activist Thich Nhat Hanh wrote, "Touch your suffering. Face it directly, and your joy will become deeper."

So let's go there. Let's dig into the tests and difficulties of life. What experiences do you find most challenging? What are your struggles trying to teach you?

What spiritual seeds of wisdom are waiting to be found as you gently, consciously take in the hard stuff we all inevitably will face?

Let's embrace our cracks so that the light can fully find its way in.

FIELD NOTES!

Saying "I Don't"
by Shabnam Mogharabi

I stared at my finger where the ring used to be. My chest was tight. I couldn't breathe.

The large, square-cut, not-my-style diamond engagement ring was gone. And I felt terrified.

I was standing in the middle of the Las Vegas Convention Center exhibit floor during a massive real estate conference. I was there for work, researching a piece on the housing crisis plaguing the country. And I was having a full-blown panic attack.

I could hear thudding in my chest. My eyes stung. I wracked my brain, trying to figure out when or where it had slipped off. Was it in the taxi I took? Did it come off when I threw away my lunch? Had it slipped off when I was shaking hands with housing officials after the keynote?

For weeks, my fiancé had been telling me to get the ring resized. I was busy with work, managing ongoing layoffs from the recession, overwhelmed by wedding prep, and it just kept falling to the bottom of my to-do list. He never offered to take another one of my rings and have this one resized to match; instead, he just kept reminding me how expensive it was and that he would hate it if I lost it.

And there I was, having lost it.

In a healthy relationship, losing an engagement ring would suck. It might be stressful . . . maybe you'd take it as a sign to find something less extravagant . . . maybe you'd have to cut your wedding budget . . . maybe you'd eventually learn to even laugh about it.

But I was not in a healthy relationship. I was in an unhealthy, controlling relationship with an older man.

I spent the next four hours ignoring my reporting responsibilities and, instead, retracing my every step. I dug in trash cans. I crawled on disgusting trade show floors. I spoke to taxi dispatchers and every maintenance worker I could find. I was drenched in sweat. The ring did not turn up.

I'll spare you the unpleasantries of the conversation that followed, the tears. But as I sat in my hotel room, deeply unhappy and nauseated, a thought formed in my head: *"This is the sign you've been wanting, needing, waiting for. This wedding shouldn't happen. This marriage shouldn't happen. End it now, before it's too late."*

In the chaos of Vegas, I went into autopilot mode with the same thought echoing: *Don't wait until it's too late.* So I flew to Los Angeles and headed straight for my long-distance fiancé's house to call off the wedding.

Every limb was tense as I told him it was over. That the loss of the ring was a sign. That I was unhappy. He was espousing apologies. I said I needed this cycle to end. Shaking, I got in my car as his temper flared. He pounded angrily on the windows as I drove away.

The next few months were some of the hardest in my life. He followed me back to the East Coast, so I called in sick to work, took a train to New York, and stayed with a friend from college until he left. His family called and left multiple messages on my phone about how embarrassing this would be. I had to tell friends that the wedding was off. I returned early gifts. Felt the financial strain of nonrefundable deposits.

And then there was the shame. The deep, overwhelming, humiliating *shame*.

I fell into a deep depression. For months, I couldn't sleep or eat. I was unfocused. I avoided every social setting and stopped talking to friends. I lost 20 pounds.

I also grappled deeply with my faith during this time. I found myself praying for hours every day . . . praying for forgiveness, for peace and guidance, for healing, for comfort. Yet I was also so angry at God. How could he take so many years away from me with that relationship? Why would he inflict so much pain on me?

Eventually, after 18 months consisting of therapy, antidepressants, a pretty dumb rebound relationship, long walks, moving across the country to San Francisco, and starting work on a little side hustle about exploring big spiritual ideas (which would later become my professional soulmate, SoulPancake), I emerged from my fog and started to engage with the world again, slowly and more cautiously.

It took time to process and accept that I needed this thing to happen to me. To jolt me out of my naivete. To give confidence to my inner voice and force me to listen to my intuition. To give me the space I needed to find joy again. To help me find my forever person . . . who (because God must have a sense of humor) also ended up being the same college friend in New York who supported me through it all.

That traumatizing period in my 20s shook me to my core. Looking back, it was also a period of painful growth. So as I look at my hand today, and the modest 1940s vintage ring that symbolizes so much of what is good in my life, I know it was necessary.

The mess does, indeed, matter.

Marginal Wisdom

"When we are no longer able to change a situation, we are challenged to change ourselves."

– Viktor E. Frankl, psychologist and Holocaust survivor

DEFINE

The First Noble Truth of the Buddha is, "Life is suffering." But why do we suffer? Are the challenges and tests you experience random and meaningless, or are you meant to learn something from them? What role do difficult experiences play in our lives? Where did your core beliefs around why we suffer originate?

> **Marginal Wisdom**
>
> "Character cannot be developed in ease and quiet. Only through experience of trial and suffering can the soul be strengthened, ambition inspired, and success achieved."
>
> – Helen Keller, author

EXPLORE

US president Theodore Roosevelt is believed to have said, "Comparison is the thief of joy." It is one of our favorite quotes of all time because of how truly universal it feels. In fact, some of our greatest tests in life will often stem from comparing our experiences to those of someone else. "Negative" feelings like jealousy or envy can become all-consuming when left to fester. Who or what do you compare yourself to? Who or what makes you feel jealousy or envy? What joys has this possibly deprived you of? Has this created any challenges for you? Could this toxic thought pattern be degrading the quality of your life?

> **Marginal Wisdom**
>
> "Our envy always lasts longer than the happiness of those we envy."
>
> – Heraclitus, ancient philosopher

ACTIVITY

THE SCARS THAT MADE ME!

*Poet Khalil Gibran once said, "Out of suffering have emerged the strongest souls; the most massive characters are seared with scars." If we are to believe that suffering can be a source of strength, let's consider celebrating the scars that made you. Write about **three** experiences of suffering that "seared" you. What were those challenges like in the moment? What qualities did you develop as a result? What did you learn about yourself, and are you ultimately grateful for it?*

1 _____

How it shaped me: _____

Express your gratitude for it: _____

2 _____

How it shaped me: _____

Express your gratitude for it: _____

3 _____

How it shaped me: _____

Express your gratitude for it: _____

★ BONUS ★

Choose one of the experiences you just wrote about on the previous page and draw your memory of the "you" before it happened and the "you" after it. Get creative about your representations.

Me "Before"

Me "After"

Marginal Wisdom

"Unless you learn to face your own shadows, you will continue to see them in others, because the world outside of you is only a reflection of the world inside of you."

– Carl Jung, psychiatrist and founder of analytical psychology

Section 10: Tests and Difficulties

ACTIVITY

MY FORGIVENESS LETTER

Sometimes, the biggest challenge in our life is not an experience but a relationship. Some of us have complicated relationships with our parents, our friends, our exes, even our children. So now, we want to turn inward and explore what it takes to forgive the people in our lives who have hurt us.

Forgiveness is really, really hard. It's a deeply personal choice that can take years to cultivate and make. And it's often an inherently spiritual act. The Bible tells us, "Do not judge, and you will not be judged. Do not condemn, and you will not be condemned. Forgive, and you will be forgiven."

Yet these days, we all seem to have forgotten how to forgive. We see forgiveness as a sign of weakness, not courage. We hold onto our grudges and resentments. We carry them for years. We respond emphatically to "an eye for an eye" style of revenge more than to a compassionate grace toward those who may have harmed us. We are simply not very good at forgiving. So let's practice! Fill in the forgiveness letter below about a difficult relationship in your life. Express yourself with abundant understanding, compassion, and love.

Dear _____ ,

What happened between us that has stayed with me is: _____
_____
_____
_____

At the time, it made me feel: _____
_____
_____
_____

Since then, it has affected me emotionally, physically, and spiritually as follows: _____
_____
_____
_____

174 *Soul Boom Workbook: Spiritual Tools for Modern Living*

I wish you understood the following about my experience: _____
_____
_____
_____

I know I need to forgive you for: _____
_____
_____
_____

I also need to forgive myself for: _____
_____
_____
_____

> **Marginal Wisdom**
>
> "As I walked out the door toward the gate that would lead to my freedom, I knew if I didn't leave my bitterness and hatred behind, I'd still be in prison."
>
> – Nelson Mandela, anti-apartheid leader and Nobel laureate

Our relationship has taught me: _____
_____
_____
_____

Now, I want to hold on to: _____
_____
_____
_____

And I want to let go of: _____
_____
_____
_____

Seeking peace, _____

EXPLORE

Cancer and other serious illnesses can be life-rattling. Yet many studies tell us that painful diagnoses often lead patients to feel more gratitude, be more present, and change their priorities. We certainly saw this with a documentary show we executive produced, My Last Days, *a series about individuals living with a terminal illness. Almost every participant we met during those hard and emotionally draining filming days was not only surprisingly hopeful, optimistic, and determined but also emotionally changed by the experience.*

Indeed, health issues can be pivotal in our lives. But maybe there is also beauty to be found in them. The COVID-19 pandemic was a universally unsettling and intense period of time, even for those who did not get seriously ill. Write about how the pandemic affected your life—socially, emotionally, spiritually. What did it take for you to survive that period of time? Did anything happen in all that quarantining and social distancing that gave you hope or made you feel grateful? If not, do you think there might ever be a time when you will look back on the experience as one that helped you grow? (Note: If you don't want to write about the pandemic, that is absolutely fine. Instead, write about a health scare you or a family member went through.)

> **Marginal Wisdom**
>
> "People have to go through trials and tribulations to get where they at. Do your thing—continue to rock it—because obviously, God wants you here."
>
> – Kendrick Lamar, rapper and musician

REFLECT

As you've been digging into all of the tests, difficulties, and hardships in your life, let's pause to consider the purpose of those challenges. Many faith traditions tell us that suffering is not only a crucial part of life but often necessary to get closer to the Divine. Read through the quotes from various religious practices below. Rank them in order of which ones speak to you most about the reason for (and meaning of) our suffering.

Religious or Spiritual Scripture	Rank 1 to 9
"This is the noble truth of suffering: Birth is suffering; aging is suffering; illness is suffering; death is suffering. . . . When one sees the helplessness in those overwhelmed by suffering, compassion arises." *Buddhism*	
"See, I have refined you, but not like silver; I have tested you in the furnaces of adversity." *Judaism*	
"He who performs good deeds in this world, in the face of adversity, shall attain the best existence." *Zoroastrianism*	
"Not only so, but we also glory in our sufferings, because we know that suffering produces perseverance; perseverance, character; and character, hope." *Christianity*	
"One whose mind remains undisturbed amidst misery, who does not crave for pleasure, and who is free from attachment, fear, and anger, is called a sage of steady wisdom." *Hinduism*	
"When we live inside our purpose, our path is smooth. When we live outside our purpose, our path is full of obstacles." *Cherokee proverb*	
"Men who suffer not, attain no perfection. The plant most pruned by the gardeners is that one which, when the summer comes, will have the most beautiful blossoms and the most abundant fruit." *Baha'i Faith*	
"Do you think you will enter Paradise without God testing those of you who fought hard and remained steadfast?" *Islam*	
"Suffering (or pain) makes the mind strong; it ushers a person to his true self within; it unites us with others; it develops the feeling of empathy and collaboration." *Sikhism*	

ACTIVITY

STICKY NOTE MARCH!

In Star Wars: Episode III—Revenge of the Sith, Yoda wisely says, "Train yourself to let go of everything you fear to lose." It's a classic Buddhist idea echoing in a galaxy far, far away. But there's truth to the power of detachment (or nonattachment). It can be freeing and transformative.

So let's give it a try! Grab a pile of Post-its. Write down all the things you feel attached to (e.g., my home, success, Mom's approval, etc.). Write down all the tests and challenges you struggle with (e.g., impatience, divorce, finances). Place the sticky notes all over your arms and legs, your chest and back. Then start walking.

Take a stroll around your home or outside. (Don't worry, after seeing you hug a tree and talk to a stone, your neighbors already know you're a bit weird.) As you move, pay attention to which notes fall off you. Can you let that attachment go? Is it serving you or better left falling away? What does it feel like to "lose" these things that weigh your mind down? Reflect on the experience here.

Marginal Wisdom

"Don't let your happiness depend on something you may lose."

– C. S. Lewis, author and theologian

ACTIVITY

MY SPIRITUAL SWOT!

In corporate settings, a SWOT analysis is often used as a strategic planning tool. Organizations identify their internal strengths (S) and weaknesses (W) and the external opportunities (O) and threats (T) that they will have to navigate. It's a tool that is helpful in identifying what a company has (or needs to develop) to create clarity and alignment before growth.

Below is a Spirituality SWOT framework. Use it to identify your inner strengths and weaknesses, the tests you face, and how you can transform them into opportunities for personal growth.

STRENGTHS — Inner qualities that help me to handle challenges

WEAKNESSES — Habits or patterns that make challenges hard for me to handle

OPPORTUNITIES — Spiritual tools (e.g., prayer, service) that might help me grow

THREATS — Tests currently threatening my ability to harness spiritual tools

Section 10: Tests and Difficulties

REFLECT

Complete this "year in review" chart. List some of the biggest tests, difficulties, challenges, hardships, and losses of that time period. What happened, and how did you overcome them? Then, celebrate the personal virtues and character traits that got you through and what you ultimately learned.

What happened?	How did I overcome it?	Which of my virtues or character traits helped me through?	What did I learn?

Marginal Wisdom

"I am ready to face any challenges that might be foolish enough to face me."

– Dwight Schrute in *The Office*

ACTIVITY

BUILD AN EMOTIONAL FIRST-AID KIT!

Suffering, pain, scars, tough relationships, illness—we've hit a bunch of the big tests we, as humans, face. Religious wisdom tells us that these challenges exist to help us seek and find the divine.

But when you're "in it," dealing with the hard stuff of life, oof ... it can be really hard to remember to center meaning in our difficulties. "I'm dealing with the biggest disappointment of my life, and you want me to reflect on the divine? Hard pass." The truth is, sometimes we need help right there, in the moment, to lift ourselves out of the darkness and remind ourselves that we have the strength to make it through.

Enter the emotional first-aid kit! It's a lifeline of sorts to bust out when you're in need of a little resilience, fortitude, and encouragement to keep going!

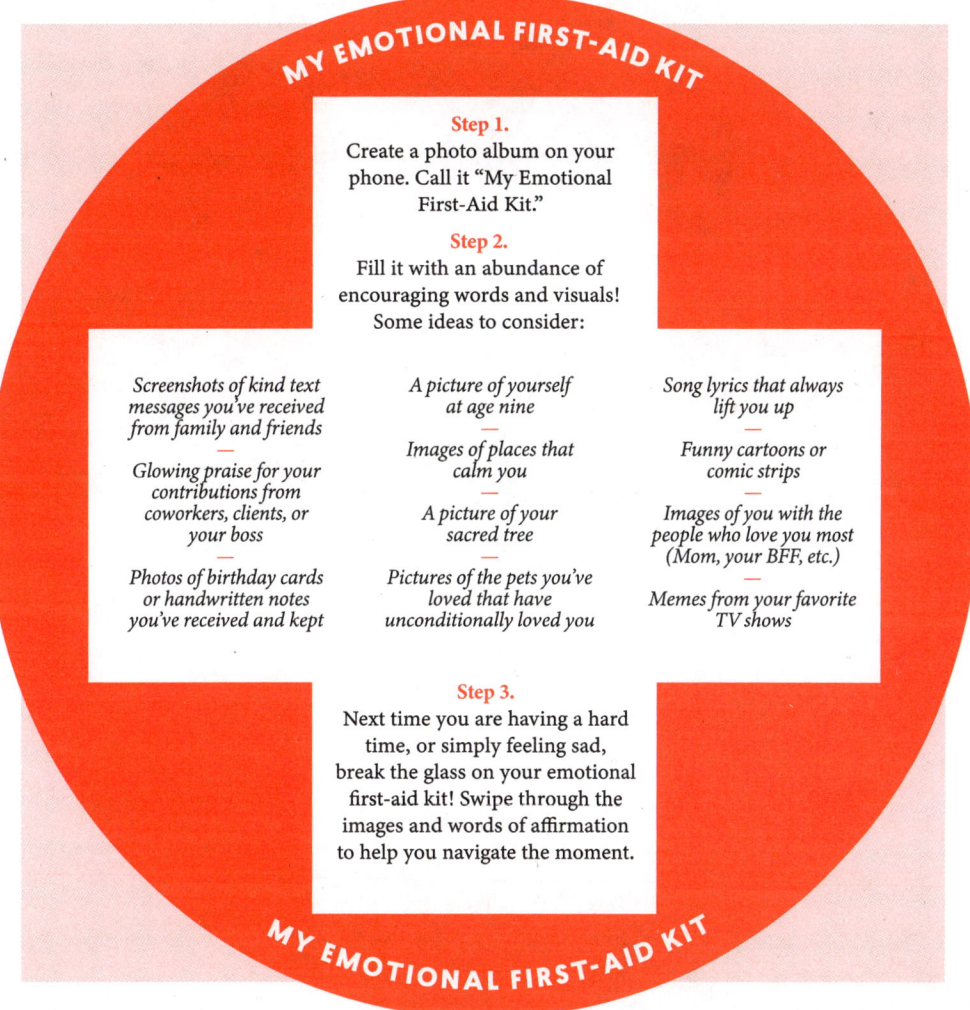

MY EMOTIONAL FIRST-AID KIT

Step 1.
Create a photo album on your phone. Call it "My Emotional First-Aid Kit."

Step 2.
Fill it with an abundance of encouraging words and visuals! Some ideas to consider:

Screenshots of kind text messages you've received from family and friends

—

Glowing praise for your contributions from coworkers, clients, or your boss

—

Photos of birthday cards or handwritten notes you've received and kept

A picture of yourself at age nine

—

Images of places that calm you

—

A picture of your sacred tree

—

Pictures of the pets you've loved that have unconditionally loved you

Song lyrics that always lift you up

—

Funny cartoons or comic strips

—

Images of you with the people who love you most (Mom, your BFF, etc.)

—

Memes from your favorite TV shows

Step 3.
Next time you are having a hard time, or simply feeling sad, break the glass on your emotional first-aid kit! Swipe through the images and words of affirmation to help you navigate the moment.

Section 10: Tests and Difficulties

Section 11

DEATH *and* DYING

HUMANS are so weird. We binge-watch horror movies where people are picked off one by one in increasingly wild and creative ways (we see you, *Final Destination*). We cheer when the villain in the Marvel movie dies. Death is great when it's fictional. But not so much when it's personal.

Interestingly, Jeffrey Reddick, creator of the *Final Destination* franchise, has said that he wrote the original film as a "meditation on death," just told through a horror genre.

Unfortunately, a deep, meaningful conversation about death is hard to have in most spaces. Death forces us to ask meaty questions about our lives and what truly matters in them. It asks us to wonder if "living life to the fullest" means sex, drugs, partying in Ibiza, or something bigger, like art, beauty, prayer.

We at *Soul Boom* believe that death is never really about dying. It's about life and living. And it's one of the most human and spiritual conversations one can have.

Every culture, community, and religion in the world wrestles with death . . . and finds fascinating ways to honor it. Egyptians stuffed tombs with snacks for the afterlife. Vikings sent bodies out to sea. Mexicans celebrate with a riot of color, marigolds, shrines, and music during Dia de los Muertos.

Comedians, the truth tellers of our time, have a particularly distinct ability to cut to the heart of the matter when it comes to grappling with death. Steven Wright, master of the one-liner, once said, "I intend to live forever. So far, so good."

And he's right. Our modern lives have developed a kind of spiritual amnesia around death. We sanitize it, hide it away, try to outwit it with antioxidants, Botox, ice baths, and biohacking.

Comedian George Carlin said, "The most unfair thing about life is the way it ends." And indeed, death is the ending to all of our stories. We spend our lives avoiding it. Or find ourselves having to deal with it when we are least prepared.

We believe that reflecting on death is the best way to connect us to life. How we approach, think about, and ponder death and dying says everything about how we also think about life.

So in this section, we're holding up a figurative mirror to one of life's biggest mysteries: death. We'll explore all the big questions: Why do we fear death? Why does reflecting on death matter? What can dying teach us about living? And what do you hope happens when you die?

FIELD NOTES!

Goodbye, Dad
By Rainn Wilson

Back in 2020, wracked with sadness, I was helping to prepare my father's dead body for burial when I remembered a well-known mystical quote from the Baha'i writings. The prophet-founder of the Baha'i Faith, Baha'u'llah, echoing a Divine voice, writes, "I have made death a messenger of joy to thee, wherefore dost thou grieve?"

This verse was one I had grown up with as a Baha'i, and it had always both puzzled and intrigued me.

Wherefore do I grieve? Because I *just lost my father whom I loved with all my heart!?* Duh! He loved and cared for me since the day I was born. Took me to soccer games and bassoon concerts and museums. Supported my career in the arts in countless ways. He had a big, beautiful heart, and for all our differences, we had an eternal bond on a foundational father-son level. His loss was absolutely devastating.

In fact, for months afterward, I would sometimes see his photo come up on my phone or look at one of his beautiful paintings on my wall and break down in heaving sobs. I missed him so much.

It was *impossible* to be thinking about death as a messenger of joy any time close to his passing. So what deeper truth might this holy writing be pointing toward? The only thing I could think of was that there must be a hereafter that is unspeakably glorious. A happy hunting ground or Valhalla, perhaps? A heaven beyond space, time, and comprehension. Something far grander than clouds and harps and halos.

As I gazed at his lifeless body, laid out on a gurney in Wenatchee, Washington, in 2020, I also remembered another spiritual teaching from the Baha'i writings—a profound and fundamental metaphor, as illustrated by 'Abdu'l-Baha, the son of Baha'u'llah: *"To consider that after the death of the body, the spirit perishes is like imagining that a bird in a cage will be destroyed if the cage is broken, though the bird has nothing to fear from the destruction of the cage. . . . Its feelings will be even more powerful, its perceptions greater, and its happiness increased."*

There it is. That must be it. There's the joy. A broken cage of the body that allows the bird of the spirit to soar, unencumbered by what's holding it back. In this case, the material limitations of the physical realm, which act like a constraint to true freedom. That poetic allusion allows the heart and mind to visualize the journey of a soul in such an infinitely inspiring way.

To be perfectly honest, it was humanly impossible to not grieve at that time. Or for the many months afterward. But over the past several years, the craziest thing has been happening: I've been getting an intangible but ever-present sense of my father on the "other side," from the plane beyond the veil.

And, at risk of sounding unbearably woo-woo, my intuition is that his essence, his spirit or soul, is indeed free. Powerful. Soaring.

And available.

I speak to him in the ether sometimes. Saying things like, "Hey, Pops, I miss you." And "Hey, Dad, can you help me out somehow with this thing I'm going through? Could really use your advice!" And "I love you, Papa."

As if he's an invisible bird somewhere up over my shoulder, flying, unhindered by his cage. And occasionally, every once in a while, I get the sense that he just might be speaking back.

> **Marginal Wisdom**
>
> "Death is no more than passing from one room into another. But there's a difference for me, you know. Because in that other room, I shall be able to see."
>
> – Helen Keller, author

DEFINE

A little over 100 years ago, 25% of babies died during childbirth. Death was a very visceral and present reality of the human experience. Today, we live longer, healthier lives, so death is less ever-present. As a result, we have stopped talking about death. We know what happens physically—our hearts stop beating, our neurons stop firing, and our bodies slowly begin to decompose. But is that all there is? Entrepreneur Steve Jobs once said, "Death is very likely the single best invention of Life. It is Life's change agent. It clears out the old to make way for the new." What's your viewpoint? Some questions to consider:

What does "death" mean to you personally? Is it an ending, a decomposition, perhaps a transition?

What does your family, faith, tradition, or culture do to deal with death (or not deal with it)?

> **Marginal Wisdom**
>
> "People are asleep. When they die, they will wake up."
>
> – Imam Ali, early Islam spiritual leader

EXPLORE

One of humanity's most universal fears is that of dying. Studies show that nearly 60% of adults report some degree of fear about their own deaths, a fear that tends to spike in midlife. For many, it's not just the end that's terrifying but also the how: the pain, the loss of control, the silence that follows. What if these fears are not a weakness but rather a signal that we are deeply, beautifully aware of how much life matters?

Below is a list of common fears about death. Select **up to five** *fears that feel most real to you. Be gentle with yourself as you sit with them—try not to think about how to overcome them. Instead, seek to* understand *what these fears are telling you.*

- ☐ I fear the unknown.
- ☐ I fear not existing or ceasing to be.
- ☐ I am afraid of feeling pain while dying.
- ☐ I am afraid of being alone when I die.
- ☐ I fear being forgotten.
- ☐ I fear leaving my loved ones behind.
- ☐ I worry about unfinished business or regrets.
- ☐ I am afraid of being judged by God.
- ☐ I worry about what comes after death.
- ☐ I am anxious about losing control.
- ☐ I fear not having lived a meaningful life.
- ☐ I worry I'll be a burden when I'm dying.
- ☐ I have anxiety about planning for death.

- ☐ I fear dying suddenly or violently.
- ☐ I fear dying slowly or without dignity.
- ☐ I worry I won't get to say goodbye.
- ☐ I don't want my loved ones to grieve.
- ☐ I fear losing my voice or essence.
- ☐ I fear that I won't leave a legacy behind.
- ☐ I fear being unprepared for death.
- ☐ I worry about the cost of my death for my loved ones.
- ☐ I'm anxious about leaving my kids alone.
- ☐ I have doubts about what I believe.
- ☐ I worry I won't reconcile with someone.
- ☐ I worry my life won't be remembered.
- ☐ Other: _____

Looking at the fears you selected, reflect below about what these fears might be telling you about the life you want to live.

_____
_____
_____
_____
_____
_____
_____
_____
_____
_____
_____

> **Marginal Wisdom**
>
> "The bitterest tears shed over graves are for words left unsaid and deeds left undone."
>
> – Harriet Beecher Stowe, author

ACTIVITY

DO A MEDI-DEATH-ATION!

One of the most well-known Tibetan practices is the "Maranasati," or death meditation. Sounds morbid, right? We promise, it's not. Rooted in Buddhism, it is intended to be a deeply spiritual reflection that helps clear us from fear around death in order to focus on what is real and important. Consider this Buddhist passage from Mahaparinibbana Sutta:

> On one occasion, the Buddha asked several of the monks, "How often do you contemplate death?"
>
> One of them replied, "Lord, I contemplate death every day."
>
> "Not good enough," the Buddha said and asked another monk, who replied, "Lord, I contemplate death with each mouthful that I eat during the meal."
>
> "Better, but not good enough," said the Buddha. "What about you?"
>
> The third monk said, "Lord, I contemplate death with each inhalation and each exhalation."

Marginal Wisdom

"Analysis of death is not for the sake of becoming fearful but to appreciate this precious lifetime."

— Dalai Lama

Numerous studies have shown that this practice of deep meditation on dying can actually increase our sense of gratitude, lead to more compassion for ourselves and others, reduce our anxiety about death and dying, support us through grief, and increase our general zest for life.

A true Maranasati requires contemplating the ever-present potential for death at any moment in order to awaken clarity and compassion around life. It can range from reflecting on the fragility and impermanence of life to a deeper contemplation on the actual visceral experience of how the body breaks down and decomposes during the dying process. In some practices, you literally visualize lying down, dirt falling upon you, your loved ones gathering around you to mourn, your body decomposing back into the earth.

Here, we've created a "starter kit" for a Maranasati-inspired meditation— one that focuses on life's impermanence, our mortality and the mortality of all things, and what that might mean for the life we want to live. Give it a try!

(1) Prepare.
Sit comfortably in a quiet place. Light a candle, if you'd like. Keep your spine straight and your body relaxed. Ground yourself with a few deep breaths. Then, bring awareness to your breathing. Feel your chest rise as you inhale deeply. Exhale slowly. Allow your mind to settle.

(2) Start with impermanence.

Repeat:	As you repeat:
"This body will not last forever. This life will not last forever."	Visualize the natural cycle of life. Birth, aging, illness, and death. Notice that every phase requires change and that the previous phase comes to an end.

(3) Contemplate your own mortality.

Repeat:	As you repeat:
"One day, I will die. I do not know when or how."	Notice what thoughts or emotions arise. Do you feel fear? Resistance? Grief? Peace? Let your feelings come. Let them go.

(4) Now think of all beings.

Repeat:	As you repeat:
"Just as I will die, so will all beings."	Think of your loved ones, your neighbors, famous and influential people, strangers, even those you dislike. Everyone shares this path. Let this awareness allow compassion for others to soften your heart.

(5) Cultivate clarity.

Repeat:	As you repeat:
"May I live with purpose. May I love fully. May I be of service before the end."	Breathe deeply in and out as you set this intention.

(6) Reflect.
Sit in silence for a moment. Now, journal below. Consider how this meditation made you feel. What emotions rose to the surface? What vulnerabilities came up as you thought deeply about death? Did this meditation make you feel gratitude for living? Describe your experience.

_____
_____
_____
_____
_____
_____

EXPLORE

Many philosophers and spiritual leaders believe the purpose of our physical reality is to prepare us for a spiritual experience in the afterlife. Do you agree? Why or why not? If there is an afterlife of some kind, would that make you more or less conscientious about your behavior and actions? Do we need an afterlife to inspire certain behaviors in people? Or has fear of hell and hoping for heaven done more harm than good over the centuries?

> **Marginal Wisdom**
>
> "Somebody should tell us, right at the start of our lives, that we are dying. Then we might live life to the limit, every minute of every day."
>
> – Pope Paul VI

ACTIVITY

BEYOND THE WOMB!

Baha'u'llah, the prophet-founder of the Baha'i Faith, wrote about death, saying, "The world beyond is as different from this world as this world is different from that of the child while still in the womb of its mother." We love this analogy. Below is a blank table. On the left-hand side, write down all the features that a baby develops inside the womb that it will not use until after it is born. On the right-hand side, write down all the spiritual/non-physical qualities we might be developing that we may not use until we reach the great beyond.

What Babies Develop That Get Used Only After Being Born	What Humans Develop That Might Get Used Only After We Die
e.g., **Eyes**—*Babies' eyes are closed in the womb until 28 weeks; even when open, there's not much to see*	e.g., **Intuition**—*Maybe we will use it to stay connected to loved ones in this "realm"*

> **Marginal Wisdom**
>
> "In life, we weep at the thought of death. In death, perhaps we weep at the thought of life."
>
> – Marilyn Monroe, actress

If you were to accept this shift in perspective—that this life is about developing qualities for another plane of spiritual existence and reality—how would that change your behavior now? What would you be motivated or encouraged to do differently?

_____

_____

_____

_____

_____

Section 11: Death and Dying

ACTIVITY

THE GAME OF (AFTER) LIFE!

In Soul Boom, Rainn talked about a classic Milton Bradley board game from his childhood, the Game of Life. It's a preposterous journey from childhood to old age in which you make stops to buy a car, get married, go to college, get a job, pay bills and taxes, and ultimately "win" by becoming a millionaire. The end.

We want to flip this idea on its head. Let's assume there is an afterlife, a next world that this world is somehow preparing us for. And let's design a new version of the Game of Life—we'll call it the Game of (After) Life—about the journey to make it to this heavenly realm. Map out what experiences, tests, virtues, qualities, and relationships you need to develop, acquire, or overcome in your one precious and beautiful existence now in order to "win" when you transition to the next world.

Draw, doodle, sketch, and color away. Get whimsical with tile names and challenges. We have given you some examples below.

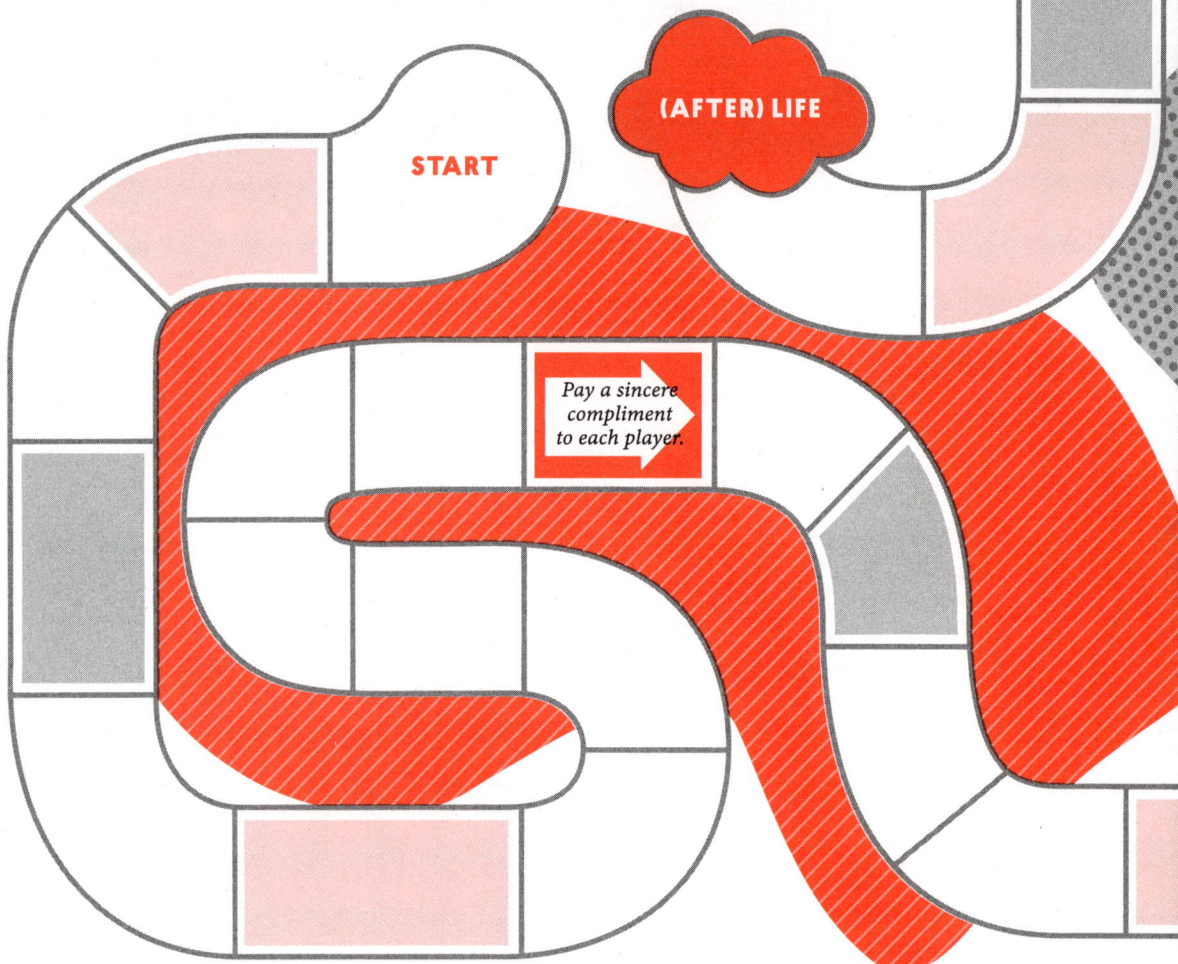

192   Soul Boom Workbook: Spiritual Tools for Modern Living

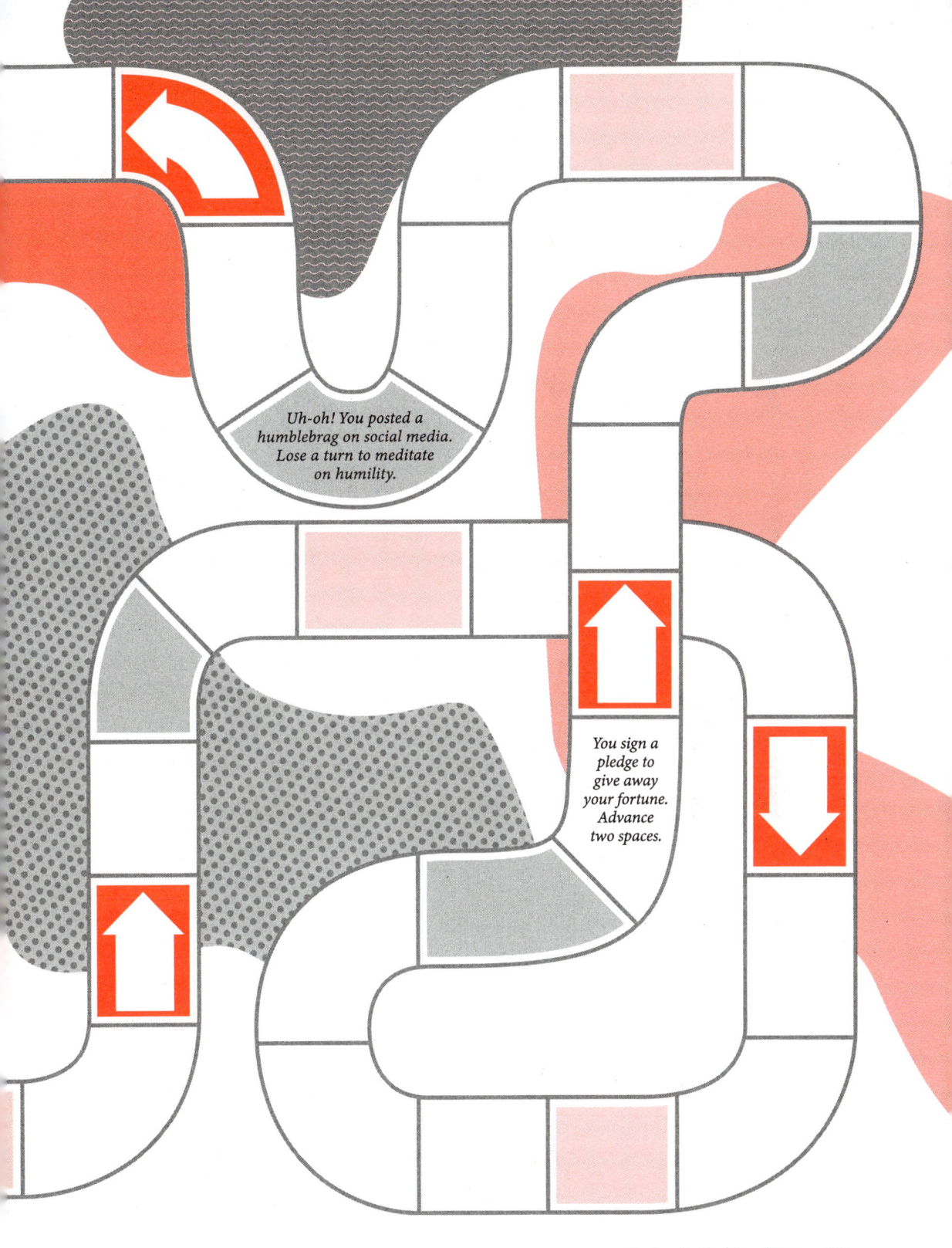

ACTIVITY

DEATH RITUALS ROUNDUP!

*The significance of death in our lives is so powerful that every civilization, society, and group has developed rituals and practices around grief. Some are spiritual in nature; others simply serve to honor the importance of death. Below is a list of 20 rituals and practices associated with grief and death from around the world. Select the **five** that most resonate with you.*

- ☐ **Axexe** *Afro-Brazilian:* A ceremony involving drumming and chanting, with specific rhythms to call forth spiritual guides and honor the life of the deceased.

- ☐ **Antyesti** *Hinduism:* The "last sacrifice" ritual where the body is cremated on a funeral pyre, followed by prayers and chants.

- ☐ **Shinso-sai** *Japanese Buddhism:* A funeral ceremony involving a purification ritual, after which the dead are enshrined as ancestral spirits and lanterns are released.

- ☐ **Dia de los Muertos** *Mexico:* A ritual of setting up altars (*ofrendas*) with marigolds, food, and music to remember and honor ancestors.

- ☐ **Keening** *Scottish:* A vocal lament performed by women to honor the dead.

- ☐ **Mallki** *Incan:* A ritual mummification and placement in sacred sites with offerings to sustain the spirit's journey.

- ☐ **Novena** *Roman Catholic:* Nine days of prayer for the soul's repose.

- ☐ **Awn** *Mapuche tribe:* A shaman-led funeral ritual to guide the soul to the afterlife and protect it from evil spirits.

- ☐ **Tangihanga** *Māori tribe:* A communal mourning ceremony with speeches, songs, and laments.

- ☐ **Anaa'ji** *Navajo tribe:* A purification ceremony to protect the community from any lingering spirits after a quick burial.

- ☐ **Ukubuyisa** *Zulu tribe:* The ritual of respectfully slaughtering an animal to cleanse the home of the deceased and honor their spirit.

- ☐ **Dama** *Mali:* A ceremony that includes masked dancers, who help guide the deceased's spirit to the afterlife.

- ☐ **Janazeh** *Islam:* A prayer performed within 24 hours of death before the body is buried facing Mecca.

- ☐ **Sky Burial** *Mongolian Buddhism:* Ritual where the body is exposed for vultures to find, showing life's impermanence.

- ☐ **Spirit Space** *Afro-American Hoodoo:* An altar with candles and offerings to maintain a connection with the spirits.

- ☐ **Irish Wake** *Irish Catholic:* A communal gathering with storytelling, music, and viewing of the body at home.

- ☐ **Marime** *Romani:* A practice where objects associated with the dead (e.g., bed, belongings) are destroyed or discarded after elaborate funerals of feasting and music.

- ☐ **Panawag-tawag** *Filipino Bukidnon tribe:* A ritual where the deceased is dressed in finery, seated in a chair, often with a lit cigarette, while visitors talk to them as if still alive.

- ☐ **Balfarar** *Viking:* A ship burial where the deceased is placed on a boat with goods, food, and weapons and sent out to sea.

- ☐ **Sagdid** *Zoroastrian:* A ritual where a sacred dog is brought to view the body, which is believed to ward off evil spirits.

Marginal Wisdom

"What is grief, if not love persevering?"

— Vision (played by Paul Bettany) in *WandaVision*

WRITE

Reflecting on the universality of death that you and all of humanity will experience is one thing. But actually losing someone you love—watching them die, realizing you will never hear their voice again, feeling the grief wash over you in surprising and heartbreaking ways—that is how many of us experience death in our lifetimes.

Writing about loss is one of the most healing rituals available to us. Grief experts often say that grief is just love with nowhere to go— so putting pen to paper gives it somewhere to land. According to research published in the Journal of Palliative Medicine, expressive writing, especially about loss, can significantly reduce symptoms of depression and post-traumatic stress while increasing resilience.

Psychologist Dr. Robert Neimeyer, who has studied grief extensively, teaches that maintaining a "continuing bond" with a loved one who has passed is not only normal but often essential for healing. Which is probably why nearly every spiritual and faith tradition teaches that our connection with the departed transcends time and space. Speaking, dreaming about, and writing to— and hearing from—a loved one can open up space for comfort, meaning, and deep reflection.

The writing activity that follows is inspired by one of our favorite poems about death, "If I Be the First of Us to Die," by novelist Nicholas Evans. It opens with the lines:

> **Marginal Wisdom**
> "Unable are the loved to die, for love is immortality."
> – Emily Dickinson, poet

If I be the first of us to die,
Let grief not blacken long your sky.
Be bold yet modest in your grieving.
There is a change but not a leaving.
For just as death is part of life,
The dead live on forever in the living.

Let's tap into the idea that the dead live on in the living. Think of someone you have lost in your life. Someone whose love is imprinted on your heart. Write a letter to that person, telling them all the things you are dealing with and struggling with in your life. What you miss about them. The questions you still have.

A LETTER TO THE DEPARTED

Dear _____ ,

_____

_____

_____

_____

_____

_____

_____

_____

_____

_____

_____

_____

_____

_____

_____

_____

_____

_____

_____

_____

_____

With all my love, _____

Now, let's turn the tables and have your loved one respond to you. Write an imagined response from the individual you wrote to on the previous page. What do you think they would say? What comforts or guidance would they offer?

A LETTER FROM THE BEYOND

Dear _____,

_____
_____
_____
_____
_____
_____
_____
_____
_____
_____
_____
_____
_____
_____
_____
_____
_____
_____
_____
_____

With all my love, _____

ACTIVITY

Research from Stanford's Life Review Project shows that reflecting on one's legacy can reduce anxiety and increase life satisfaction, especially when paired with storytelling or a spiritual practice. When we imagine how we want to be remembered, we uncover what truly matters. It's usually not our job title; it's our kindness. It's not our possessions but the people we love and who love us back. Below, write a eulogy for yourself about your most meaningful life and how you want to be remembered.

This is a eulogy for: _____

They would want to be remembered for: _____

_____

_____

_____

_____

The people they loved with wild abandon were: _____

_____

_____

_____

_____

Their greatest passions and pursuits in life were: _____

_____

_____

_____

_____

They impacted the lives of others by: _____

_____

_____

_____

_____

They believed deeply in: _____

_____

_____

_____

_____

A story that really captures who they were is: _____

_____

_____

_____

_____

> **Marginal Wisdom**
>
> "The art of living well and the art of dying well are one."
>
> – Epicurus, ancient philosopher

They lived by the following values and principles: _____

_____

_____

_____

_____

They always made people around them feel: _____

_____

_____

_____

_____

Their final message to the world would probably be: _____

_____

_____

_____

_____

Section 12

The
MEANING
of
LIFE

ANXIETY. Loneliness. Pain. Suffering. Dying. Death.

We have hit all the hard things, haven't we? So now we want to take a step back. To find the light and uplift in all of this heaviness. And to explore perhaps the biggest question of all:

Why am I here, and what does it all mean?

When we're suffering or in pain, we wonder why it's happening. When we're rushing through life, building and loving and sacrificing our way through our days, we want to believe that it matters. That it is part of something bigger. That it has *meaning*.

At *Soul Boom*, we believe meaning quietly shapes everything. In fact, purpose is a central idea in every spiritual practice. The Bible opens with the intentional and purposeful act of creation. Indigenous spiritual leaders remind us that purpose is not individual but rather a collective expression of community and land. And we believe that there is power in knowing the "meaning" of life . . . not just in the grandiose sense of the meaning of *all* life but also in understanding and fulfilling the meaning of your own individual life.

We like how psychiatrist and Holocaust survivor Viktor Frankl puts it: "Life is never made unbearable by circumstances, but only by lack of meaning." In fact, his greatest work, *Man's Search for Meaning*, has inspired decades of research on how purpose can sustain us.

Modern science backs him up. A 2014 study published in *The Journal of Psychological Science* found that people with a strong sense of purpose lived longer, regardless of age, gender, or emotional state. A 2020 study from *JAMA Psychiatry* showed that people with a higher sense of meaning had significantly lower risk of depression, addiction, and suicide.

In other words, knowing your *why* influences your ability to manage the *how* of your life.

Which means the opposite is likely true, too. A lack of meaning can leave us restless, numb, or grasping for things that fill our time but don't necessarily nourish us—status, wealth, highs, orgasms, clicks, likes, distractions. (America, in a nutshell.)

Like most hard things, finding meaning takes a whole ton of work. It's a layered, nuanced clawing open of your soul and the life you live. It can show up in parenting, in painting, in protest. In quiet acts of kindness or in big, loud revolutions.

This section will help you explore where meaning already lives in your life— and where it's waiting to be invited in. So let's get started.

FIELD NOTES!

What "Brandon" Believes
By Shabnam Mogharabi

All humans want something to believe in—deeply, fully, viscerally believe in.

I internalized this idea while running our mission-driven content studio, SoulPancake. We accomplished so many beautiful and amazing things (1 billion video views! Meeting Oprah!), and I have learned over the years that it wasn't because of any specific talents or people. It was because of our *why*. We assembled a team of people who truly *believed* in the change we wanted to create in the world. Who wanted to make inspiring content for and about humanity.

They were Pancakes for life, and they had bought into our mission. It was intoxicating to be at SoulPancake during those early years. We all felt afire with dedication—we were determined to bring our POV to the world. Because how could *everyone* not want to experience this joyful, uplifting magic?

But having something to believe in can serve darker means as well. In *Soul Boom*, Rainn told the story of one instance of a young, white man who engaged with our content. It bears retelling because it is so central to this discussion about belief and purpose.

Our social media managers at SoulPancake had clear policies about how and when we would engage with our fans. We always encouraged users to "speak your mind, but don't hit below the belt." We would answer questions about the videos. We would thumbs-up any insightful comments or rising compliments.

And we would delete hateful comments and slurs. (You'd be surprised, for instance, to know how many awful, cruel comments were posted on Kid President videos about the sweet, innocent *child* who played this character. We deleted them all, as we never wanted him to grow up and see them.)

One time, we posted a video with black participants talking about what it was like to grow up black in America. They described how they believe the world sees them. In the comments, one response went "viral" with activity. A young, white man, whom I will call Brandon for the purposes of this, posted this comment:

> **@Brandon** 23 minutes ago
> Can someone tell me why I'm supposes to have privilige? I only have ever been called white trash since I was a little kid. Me and my mom live in a trailer park. I work at Dairy Queen. She doesn't even work because of her diabetus but I'm supposes to have privilige. I know more black people with privilige than I have.
>
> 👍 23   👎 500   **Reply**
>
> ⌄ **326 replies**

The response from the audience was anything but understanding. Some responded, telling Brandon, "You are the problem." Others wrote multiple paragraphs about the history of white supremacy and his complicity in it. Brandon tried once to explain himself, and the first response was: "RACIST!"

Our social media manager at the time brought this conversation to my attention. She was concerned that he was being shunned and disrespected. She didn't know what to do. I suggested she remove the comments that were attacking Brandon or were rude. But I said that we don't really get involved in the discussions themselves.

My advice was wrong. I made a terrible mistake in judgment.

I should have told our social media manager to reach out privately to Brandon. To engage him in a loving, polite conversation. To "call him in" instead of letting the social media masses call him out, as Loretta J. Ross, a feminist and professor at Smith College, once eloquently articulated.

What happened next still haunts me to this day.

Marginal Wisdom

"Dying for something is easy because it is associated with glory. Living for something is the hard thing. Living for something extends beyond fashion, glory, or recognition. We live for what we believe."

– Donald Miller in *Blue Like Jazz: Nonreligious Thoughts on Christian Spirituality*

Section 12: The Meaning of Life

Quickly and quietly, several users began directly responding to Brandon, saying things like "See? These people will never understand you. They think anyone who is white is evil." Or comments like "We know your life is hard. There are lots of people who feel like you."

And as Brandon engaged with them, they started sharing links, expertly guiding him to conspiracy theory websites, alt-right podcasts, and dark web communities. We tried to catch the links where we could and delete them, but it was like playing whack-a-mole.

Eventually, Brandon's comments became volatile, violent, and racist. One day, he stopped posting comments on SoulPancake videos altogether. He deleted his profile.

He was gone. He had turned into an "angry white man" right before our eyes. And I let it happen.

I still carry a lot of guilt for not intervening in a different way. For not inviting this naive, young soul into a different conversation. One that focused on unity and our common human destiny.

Brandon needed meaning in his life. He was suffering, and he wanted to talk about it. He wanted to belong, but he felt alone. And then "they" found him. And they gave him meaning and purpose inside a racist ideology.

Like I said, all humans want something to believe in—deeply, fully, viscerally believe in. So if we're going to succeed in launching a modern spiritual revolution, we are going to need to "call in" everyone with love. To let go of our knee-jerk judgments and steer people toward the good and the light. No matter what their background. No matter how different they may seem. No matter where we need to meet them.

DEFINE

If you had to give an answer right this second, what would you define as the "meaning of life"? And do you believe it matters? Have your perspectives been shaped by the world and people around you—your work, school, church, family, friends? Or do your beliefs stem from somewhere else—from within, from something existential? Freewrite below.

MEANING OF LIFE: GO!

> **Marginal Wisdom**
>
> "Love is our true destiny. We do not find the meaning of life by ourselves alone—we find it with another."
>
> – Thomas Merton, monk and theologian

EXPLORE

While the concepts of "meaning" and "purpose" are often used interchangeably, psychologists differentiate between them because it's only when they intertwine that they can provide a cohesive framework for our lives. This activity gives you space to explore the things that give your life meaning and purpose, as defined below.

Meaning

comes from the things that give our life significance. It provides our *WHY*.

For some, that can be the feeling they get when they create something beautiful or make someone laugh. For others, it's their deep faith in Christian love, defined in their Catholic church. Maybe for you, it's the joy of spending as much time as possible with your parents. It's the thing that we feel moves us and radiates internally.

10 Things That Give My Life MEANING or Significance—My WHYs

- _____
- _____
- _____
- _____
- _____
- _____
- _____
- _____
- _____
- _____

Purpose

gives a sense of direction to our choices and goals. It is the *WHAT* and *HOW* that our *WHY* compels us to do.

It's the drive you put into organizing protests or volunteering. Why? Because you get meaning from seeing justice in action. Purpose is giving up your career to become a stay-at-home mom. Why? Because your teen is struggling, and his thriving is what matters to you most.

10 Things That Give My Life PURPOSE or Direction—My WHATs and HOWs

- _____
- _____
- _____
- _____
- _____
- _____
- _____
- _____
- _____
- _____

How connected do your sources of meaning and purpose feel right now? Was one list easier to write and think of than the other? Do you feel more connected to the things that bring meaning or purpose to your life right now? Why do you think that is?

> **Marginal Wisdom**
>
> "Know what sparks the light in you so that you, in your own way, can illuminate the world."
>
> – Oprah Winfrey, TV host and producer

ACTIVITY

THE POWER OF PURPOSE!

Time to get practical. In the last exercise, you identified the various sources of meaning and purpose in your life. Now, it's time to connect the dots between them. In psychology, this is a field called Meaningful Purpose Psychology (MPP). In MPP theory, purpose fulfills meaning. So let's write some meaningful purpose statements!

BE SURE TO CONSIDER:

WHAT:
What do you do, and how do you do it?

WHO:
For whom? Yourself? Or other beneficiaries?

WHY:
What mission, values, or beliefs underlie these actions?

SOME EXAMPLES:

I work as a special ed teacher to teach life skills (**WHAT**) to disabled students (**WHO**) because I believe all kids deserve love (**WHY**).

I play the guitar any chance I get (**WHAT**) to help soothe my own anxiety (**WHO**) because I value music's healing powers (**WHY**).

Write a meaningful purpose statement for your career / work: _____
_____
_____

Write a meaningful purpose statement for your family life: _____
_____
_____

Write a meaningful purpose statement for a personal interest or hobby you have:
_____
_____

Write a meaningful purpose statement for your friendships or social life:
_____
_____

> **Marginal Wisdom**
>
> "It is not what we get. But who we become, what we contribute . . . that gives meaning to our lives."
>
> – Tony Robbins, author and motivational speaker

Now consider the statements you wrote. Which feels most resonant with who you are and the life you're living right now? Reflect below.
_____
_____
_____
_____
_____

EXPLORE

In many parts of the world, people find significance and meaning in their faith practices and spiritual lives. Things like the worship they undertake, or the communities they are a part of, or the compassion that's generated by engaging in service work. If you have a spiritual or faith practice, does it provide a sense of purpose for you? If not, consider that in the past few sections, you've dug into the concepts of the soul, God, values, beauty, and nature. How have those explorations influenced your view on the role religion and spirituality might play in living a life of meaning?

> **Marginal Wisdom**
>
> "The secret is not to find the meaning of life, but to use your life to make things that are meaningful."
>
> – Chidi Anagonye (played by William Jackson Harper) in *The Good Place*

REFLECT

Below are 10 quotes from religious or spiritual traditions about the purpose of life, many of which center on the acceptance and worship of God. Read through the quotes below and consider which most resonate with you. Circle, annotate, and write notes in the margins on how each one makes you feel.

"'Love the Lord your God with all your heart and with all your soul and with all your mind.' This is the first and greatest commandment. And the second is like it: 'Love your neighbor as yourself.' All the Law . . . hang on these two commandments."
—**Matthew 22:37, Christianity**

"Umuntu ngumuntu ngabantu."
Translation: "A person is a person through other people."
—**Zulu proverb on Ubuntu philosophy**

"By effort and heedfulness, discipline and self-mastery, let the wise one make for himself an island which no flood can overwhelm."
—**Dhammapada 2:25, Buddhism**

"The Peacemaker taught that the Good Mind should be used to promote peace and unity among the people."
—**Iroquois oral tradition**

"I did not create [mankind] except to worship Me."
—**Quran 51:56, Islam**

"This life is the time for men to prepare to meet God."
—**Alma 34:32, The Book of Mormon**

"The ignorant work for their own profit . . . the wise work for the welfare of the world, without thought for themselves."
—**Bhagavad Gita 3:25, Hinduism**

"Thou hast created me to know Thee and to worship Thee."
—**A Baha'i prayer**

"And what does the Lord require of you but to do justice, to love kindness, and to walk humbly with your God?"
—**Micah 6:8, The Hebrew Bible**

"Realization of Truth is higher than all else. Higher still is truthful living. . . . He alone is a man of true religion who lovingly engages in the service of others."
—**Guru Granth Sahib 62 and 1013, Sikhism**

WRITE

Soul Boom *friend Varun Soni, the dean of religious life at the University of Southern California, has said that he believes young adults today are experiencing a "modern crisis of meaning," and it is this crisis that has contributed to the global decline of mental well-being. Have you ever struggled with meaninglessness in your life? What did you turn to (reflections, actions, or even vices) when your life felt meaningless? What filled the void? Explore how you navigated this struggle and what helped you get through it.*

> **Marginal Wisdom**
>
> "He who has a why to live can bear almost any how."
>
> – Friedrich Nietzsche, philosopher

ACTIVITY

BE ALIVE!

Often, when we talk about the meaning of life, it can be a pretty intellectual, brainy sort of exercise. Author Joseph Campbell once said, "I don't believe people are looking for the meaning of life as much as they are looking for the experience of being alive." That feels pretty practical to us! After all, every cell in your body comes alive when you jump into cold ocean water. The smell of cooking a favorite family recipe can transport you back to an idyllic childhood memory.

*List **five** things you do—or want to do—that would give you the experience or sensation of being vibrantly and invigoratingly alive.*

1. _____
2. _____
3. _____
4. _____
5. _____

Now, pick one of the above activities that you think might be able to regularly give you a sense of meaning. For one week, give yourself that gift. Find time every day to commit more time and energy toward it. Journal about the experience here.

> **Marginal Wisdom**
>
> "Don't ask what the world needs. Ask what makes you come alive, and go do it. Because what the world needs is people who have come alive."
>
> – Howard Thurman, theologian and civil rights leader

EXPLORE

So many times, we find that our cloud of fears, overwhelms, and limiting beliefs holds us back from living our richest possible life. Imagine that one day, all of your internal anxieties and external expectations (e.g., fear of failure, money issues, societal pressures) completely evaporate. All the obstacles that weigh you down are lifted.

Now, explore how you might live your life differently and how you might spend your time when freed from these burdens. Some questions to consider:

How would you feel internally once liberated? Would your external behavior change?

Are there any practices, hobbies, or new routines you would seek to establish?

Where would you want to live, work, worship, and play?

Whom would you choose to spend your time with?

> **Marginal Wisdom**
>
> "How liberating it is to pursue wholeness instead of perfection."
>
> – Morgan Harper Nichols, artist and poet

ACTIVITY

TRY A JOY HACK!

Philosophy professor Roger Berkowitz recently wrote in The Times Union *a poetic passage about the darkness of our current times and what might actually be at play. He said:*

> *"What darkens our times is not only political cruelty or illiberalism. It is something deeper: a spiritual flattening of life. In our institutions, efficiency replaces justice. Art is reduced to ideology. The humanities are dismissed as impractical. The soul is neglected. Could it be that what we lack is not simply resistance, but joy?*
>
> *Joy is not happiness. It is deeper, riskier, and more transformative. Joy erupts in a lover's gaze, in Beethoven's late sonatas, in the embrace of a once-wayward child. It is not escape but a visceral affirmation of what matters most. Where happiness can be private, joy demands connection: to others, to meaning, to the world."*

We love this. But finding and cultivating joy feels, well, tough. Thankfully, there are hacks for that! Jancee Dunn, a wellness reporter for The New York Times, *recently compiled some of the best advice she's ever heard for finding happiness. Below are three of our favorites. Pick* **one** *and try it out.*

Option 1:
Start a weird ritual.

In nearly every spiritual tradition, rituals are a gateway to mindfulness. And small and strange rituals can add levity and meaning to our daily life, according to behavioral scientist Michael Norton. Rituals can turn ordinary moments into sacred ones. In fact, there's a viral social trend where women share quirky rituals to make life more whimsical, and it's delightful. So give it a try! Announce to your dishes every night that it's bath time. Kiss your cat on both cheeks and tell your friends he's French. Pick something you do every day and turn it into a consistent, silly, and weird ritual!

Option 2:
Hang out with some "yutes."

In all spiritual practices, connecting with youth reminds us of our own spiritual potential. Nonagenarian Margareta Magnusson told Dunn that being around youth always offers her a fresh perspective, and hearing their ideas "is a way to stay in tune with the young person you yourself were at some point." So find some young people! (If you're young yourself, consider volunteering some time to kids in your community.) Sign up for a community college class. Open your backyard to a local faith-based youth group. Offer them food. Listen. Ask questions. Drink from the fountain of their youth!

Option 3:
Spread "positive gossip."

All spiritual practices tell us that gossip is harmful. The Bible warns: "A gossip betrays a confidence." But what if you flipped this idea on its head? Jamil Zaki, director of Stanford's Social Neuroscience Lab, suggests spreading "positive gossip" about others. Saying good things behind someone's back isn't just kind—it's karma and good vibes! So learn a cool fact about someone and tell a mutual friend! Reshare a LinkedIn post about your colleague's promotion and rave about them. Create a ripple of positive waves around you!

Which joy hack did you choose, and why? How did you feel after trying it out? More purposeful? More connected? Reflect on the activity below. Consider going back and trying the others at a later time.

> **Marginal Wisdom**
>
> "Joy gives us wings! In times of joy our strength is more vital, our intellect keener, and our understanding less clouded."
>
> – 'Abdu'l-Baha, Baha'i central figure and spiritual leader

ACTIVITY

PLAN A $1 BILLION YEAR!

*Imagine you have $1 billion, and all your personal wants and needs are met (and then some). You can't invest it or save it or leave it all to your kids. In fact, you find out that you have only **one year** to spend it. Fill in this road map to explore the who, what, where, and why of your spending spree.*

I. MY VALUES

Before I start spending, the three values that will guide how I spend this money are:

- _____
- _____
- _____

If this money were going to send a message to the world, it would say:

_____
_____
_____

II. WHO WOULD BENEFIT?

People I personally know: _____
_____
_____
_____

Communities or causes I care about: _____
_____
_____
_____

Systems that need support: _____
_____
_____
_____

Global issues I want to impact: _____
_____
_____
_____

III. WHAT WOULD THIS CREATE?

Ultimately, I would want to see the following transformation happen: _____

_____
_____
_____
_____

I would also create one joyful, imaginative project just for fun in the form of: _____

_____
_____
_____
_____

IV. REFLECTION

After spending all of this money, I hope I would feel more:

☐ Connected	☐ Important	☐ Grounded	☐ Other: _____
☐ Free	☐ Generous	☐ Purposeful	☐ Other: _____
☐ Aligned	☐ Creative	☐ Compassionate	☐ Other: _____

If I accomplish only one thing with my $1 billion, it would be: _____

_____
_____
_____
_____
_____
_____
_____

> **Marginal Wisdom**
>
> "Attention, on the other hand, just is life: your experience of being alive consists of nothing other than the sum of everything to which you pay attention."
>
> – Oliver Burkeman in *Four Thousand Weeks: Time Management for Mortals*

★ BONUS ★

Let's see how close to your values your spending currently falls! Open up your credit card or checking account statement from the last month. Take a read through what's there. What did you spend your discretionary money on in the past 30 days? Does your spending align with your values? Note: This is not a budgeting exercise. It's a way to gauge if "hypothetical billionaire" you aligns with "actual income" you.

ACTIVITY

A LETTER TO MYSELF!

The sources of meaning in our lives often evolve over time. In fact, wisdom is just that—the discernment and insight that comes with age or experience that allows us to make sound judgments and navigate complex, nuanced situations. So let's imagine what having meaning in your life might look like in your future. Complete this letter from your wisest 90-year-old self. Address it to yourself right now, in the present moment.

Dear Me, age _____ ,

Right now, it might feel like your life (and all of your time) is spent on:
_____
_____

Most days, the feelings and challenges you struggle most with are:
_____

> **Marginal Wisdom**
>
> "Sixty years ago I knew everything; now I know nothing; education is a progressive discovery of our own ignorance."
>
> – Will Durant, historian and philosopher

It may not always be this way. By the time you are 90, you will have learned that:
_____
_____

These days, it is the people in your life who are most influenced by you. Your impact is felt by:
_____
_____

In fact, by the time you're my age, you will spend most of your time doing what you love most, which is:
_____
_____

Now, at the end of your life, the wishes you have and the things that give you the most meaning are:
_____
_____
_____

All my love,
Me, age 90

REFLECT

TAKE TWO! MEANING OF LIFE... AGAIN.

At the beginning of this section, we asked you to freewrite about the meaning of life, as you believed it to be. Have your thoughts evolved on what the meaning of life—or at least your life—might be? What feels different? What feels affirmed for you?

> **Marginal Wisdom**
>
> "There is only one meaning of life: the act of living itself."
>
> – Erich Fromm, social psychologist

★ BONUS ★

Time to do something scary, but meaningful! Call someone you care about. Don't text! Share with them some of the thoughts that you've outlined in this chapter. Describe what gives your life purpose. Tell them what you think the meaning of life might be and ask them for their definition. We promise it will pay off!

PAUSE & PONDER

We know this third unit was tough. Maybe it felt like therapy. Maybe it was cathartic. Maybe you needed to step away. But our goal was to help you root into the hard and important parts of life and how spirituality can shape them. We explored spiritual solutions to find mental well-being and manage anxiety; we worked through how to handle the tests that life throws our way; we grappled with the ultimate "ending" of life and what death might mean; and we dug into the meaning of it all.

Take a minute to flip back through the pages of Part Three. Reflect on your journey thus far below.

What was your favorite writing prompt, reflection, or activity? Why? What did it reveal about yourself?

Which prompt, reflection, or activity was the most challenging for you or made you the most uncomfortable? Why do you think that is?

As you head into the final part, which explores how spirituality might change the world, what are your biggest takeaways from this unit of work?

Draw, doodle, or sketch any final images that pop into your head as you move forward on your spiritual journey.

USE THIS SPACE TO CONTINUE EXPLORING!

Part

FOUR

Section 13:
Creating Community

Section 14:
A Service Mindset

Section 15:
How to Change the World

Soul Boom in Society

In Which We Build a Better World

Section 13

CREATING COMMUNITY

GUESS what? It's time to . . . *drum roll, please* . . . build a better world!

We know what you're thinking: How on Earth will my newfound personal spiritual understanding and all this ancient wisdom I've been exploring help me solve problems of inequality, injustice, and hate? Polarization? Political divides? War? Poverty? Immigration? Women's rights? Climate change? What the actual what?!

Volumes of books have been written about how spiritual ideas can inspire action to change the world. However, that was never the purpose of this book. Our goal was to help you explore your inner life and offer spiritual tools for modern living. But we also didn't want to *not* go there. So in this unit of work, we hope to share some ideas to get you started on unleashing a spiritual revolution in the world around you.

Our starting point is something that we believe is profoundly powerful in the quest to change the world. We want to talk about the importance of building community.

In 2025, *The New York Times* journalist Lauren Jackson embarked on writing a series called "Believing" about faith and spirituality in America. In her explanation of why she was doing this reporting, she wrote, "Religion offers people three Bs: *beliefs* about the world, *behaviors* to follow, and *belonging* in a community or culture."

The majority of this workbook has focused on exploring your beliefs and behaviors. But in this section, we will talk heavily about that third B—belonging.

Belonging is not just found by attending church potlucks and college reunions. Yes, our relationships—and how we gather with those people—are often the building blocks of community. But we want to look beyond the casseroles and cookouts. We want to dig into what is sacred about community building and feeling a sense of belonging, especially in our hyper individualistic, selfie-oriented lives.

Loneliness and antisocial behaviors are increasingly affecting every generation and country in the world. Every industry is actively trying to isolate us. To have us get into self-driving cars or engage blindly with strangers via a screen.

Yet we thrive most when we belong. And we literally suffer when we don't.

Humans are biologically wired for connection. According to Harvard University's Grant Study, the longest longitudinal study on well-being ever conducted, the single greatest predictor of human happiness and longevity comes down to the quality of our relationships. And multiple studies have shown that being friendless is worse for your health than lighting up a pack of cigarettes. Let that sink in!

All ancient spiritual wisdom affirms this. Buddhists take refuge in their *sangha*, their spiritual community. Indigenous ceremonies are almost always communal—drumming, dancing, singing *together*. The early, formative years of 18th-century America were wholly centered around the community that sprung from the local congregational church.

Spiritual teacher Ram Dass once said, "We're all just walking each other home." That's it. That's the entire mission statement! Not to outperform or outcompete. But to accompany. To witness. To make others feel less alone.

At *Soul Boom*, we believe building meaningful communities is one of the most radical spiritual acts we can commit. But here's the hard part: Community should *not* be comfortable. Belonging does not mean hanging out only with people who agree with you on everything and pronounce "aunt" the same way as you. Community requires patience, compassion, and compromise. It makes you curious, reveals your blind spots, and challenges your beliefs. True belonging, as social psychologist and author Brené Brown puts it, "doesn't require you to change who you are; it requires you to be who you are."

When we connect and commune and gather—not just physically but also soulfully—we are reminded that we are not the center of the universe, nor are we alone in it.

It's the entire foundation upon which we can build a better world. Together.

FIELD NOTES!

Let Empathy Fly
by Shabnam Mogharabi

A few months before the COVID-19 pandemic, in November 2019, Rainn and I spoke together in front of about 1,500 students at California State University in Long Beach. We often speak at college campuses together—it's a group that is eager to hear our experiences, laughs at our jokes (OK, *Rainn's* jokes), and resonates with our message.

On this particular night, we decided to do a paper airplane activity called "Let Empathy Fly" with the audience. Everyone received a piece of paper. On one side were instructions on how to fold a classic paper airplane. On the other side were two questions:

1. What has been one of the most painful struggles you've experienced?
2. What has brought you the most joy in your life?

We asked these young college students to anonymously write down their answers, fold up the paper airplanes, and after a dramatic countdown, send them flying across the auditorium. When the last airplane had fluttered to the ground and the phones had stopped recording, we asked them to pick up a nearby airplane, read what was written, and raise their hand if they resonated or connected with what they saw.

More than half the students had their hands up.

"Who is willing to share?" Rainn asked.

One by one, students read off the struggles of mental health and anxiety, being away from home, academic struggles, financial stress, health issues, and the like that their classmates suffered from. The whole audience was nodding and agreeing. The collective compassion was palpable. They were not as alone as they may have felt.

And then they started sharing their joys. Some students read about the joys of creative pursuits—writing, music, art. Others wrote about living near the water, being active, a love of travel. But for the vast majority, the answers to the "joy" question were almost always about people.

My family. My sister. My best friend. My kid. My roommate. My book club. My bandmates.

Cal State Long Beach is not an anomaly. This happens nearly every time we speak to college students. We always hear the same concerns again and again.

Everyone I know is lonely or anxious.

It's really hard to make friends.

I don't know what I want to do with my life.

The world feels pretty hopeless.

I am stressed out and overwhelmed.

I feel sad a lot.

Yet they don't realize that all around them, people are dealing with similar struggles. They already belong more than they think they do.

Now this was all BEFORE the pandemic. Before anxiety and isolation numbers skyrocketed. Before people drew inward and became more insular. Before clubs and movie theaters and churches and all the other places people gather saw their numbers dwindle.

Those college students are now in their early postcollege careers. I often wonder if, as they navigate through the ups and downs of life, they ever think back on a little paper airplane activity that the guy from *The Office* and a girl whose name they couldn't pronounce led at their school.

I hope it might occasionally seep into their subconscious and remind them that if they are willing to take a chance, open up, and join something, they might find the connection they need.

Marginal Wisdom

"We have all known the long loneliness, and we have learned that the only solution is love and that love comes with community."

– Dorothy Day, Catholic activist

DEFINE

In its simplest form, a "community" is a group of people you're connected to, and "belonging" is the feeling of being accepted, valued, and safe within that group. When you think of "community," what comes to mind? What does community bring to your life? Are you drawn to groups with shared values? Interests? Experiences? Goals? Have you ever felt disconnected from a community you belong to? What emotions make you feel like you belong? Explore your ideas and thoughts here.

> **Marginal Wisdom**
>
> "Community is society with a human face, the place where we know we are not alone."
>
> – Rabbi Jonathan Sacks, Orthodox rabbi and theologian

Section 13: Creating Community

EXPLORE

Social psychologist Brené Brown has some great gems of wisdom in this field of work! Brown defines belonging as "the innate human desire to be part of something larger than us." This important idea is also really good for us. In 2018, the UCLA Loneliness Study linked feelings of belonging with increased resilience and lower stress.

So let's explore this idea of community and how it currently shows up in your personal life. Take some time to map out and identify below the specific groups that have shaped or influenced you. (If you can't think of a match, feel free to skip it and move on to the next one.) Write about each community and then give yourself a "belonging" score for each.

WRITE ABOUT...		SENSE OF BELONGING 1 (low)—10 (high)
A community that has always been there for me:	Score:	Why this score:
A community I belong to only out of a sense of obligation:	Score:	Why this score:
A community I loved being part of when I was a kid:	Score:	Why this score:
A community that made my adolescence amazing:	Score:	Why this score:

WRITE ABOUT . . .	SENSE OF BELONGING 1 (low)—10 (high)	
A community that is centered around a place (e.g., school, gym, work):	Score:	Why this score:
A community that fulfills my spiritual needs:	Score:	Why this score:
A community I admire or aspire to from a distance:	Score:	Why this score:
A community I could really use in my life right now:	Score:	Why this score:
A community I miss or have fallen out of touch with:	Score:	Why this score:

> **Marginal Wisdom**
>
> "Sometimes the most ordinary things could be made extraordinary, simply by doing them with the right people."
>
> – Nicholas Sparks, novelist and screenwriter

ACTIVITY

COMMUNITY RECONNECT!

We just asked you to think about a community you miss or have fallen out of touch with. Think about the people who made up that group. Now, pick one of those people—ideally, someone whom you have not spoken to in the past six months. Reach out and tell them you've been thinking of them. Better yet, give them a call.

Share a photo or memory of the time you spent together and what you appreciate about them. Ask them a thoughtful or meaningful question about their life now.

When the reconnect is over, write about the experience below.

Whom did you reach out to, and why? _____

_____

_____

_____

> **Marginal Wisdom**
>
> "The essence of trauma is disconnection from the self and others. The healing of trauma is reconnection—with the self and with others."
>
> – Gabor Maté, physician and author

What memory did you share with them? _____

_____

_____

_____

What did you learn about their life now? _____

_____

_____

_____

_____

How did it feel to relive that experience and reconnect with this person? _____

_____

_____

_____

_____

DRAW

Think back to a time when you felt extremely connected to others. Maybe it was a family game night. A volunteer trip. A giant music festival in the desert. Try to recall all the details of this moment in time. Where were you? Who was there? Draw yourself in that experience and visually re-create its sights, smells, and emotions. Bring the feeling of connection to life with your sketch.

> **Marginal Wisdom**
>
> "The greatness of a community is most accurately measured by the compassionate actions of its members."
>
> – Coretta Scott King, author and civil rights activist

Section 13: Creating Community

ACTIVITY

OFRENDA OF INFLUENCE!

During Dia de los Muertos, many Mexican and Indigenous cultures create an ofrenda, *an altar that honors and remembers ancestors who have passed. We want you to honor this sacred tradition by creating an Ofrenda of Influence below. Instead of listing long-gone family members, we will focus on people who have influenced your life along its journey—the community of people from your past who have paved the way for your community today.*

On the opposite page, *you'll build this pyramid from the bottom to the top, imagining each layer as a foundation of support. (Consider revisiting the people you admired on* page 119*). Write down those who come to mind for each category, the impact they've had on you, lessons they've taught you, ways they've influenced you, and how they've shaped your sense of community today.*

Once you've completed your pyramid, *reflect below on the people in it. Which group of people was the most challenging to identify? Which category feels the richest? Are there any common themes or lessons among them? How have these invisible threads formed the community you have now?*

> **Marginal Wisdom**
>
> "There can be no vulnerability without risk; there can be no community without vulnerability; there can be no peace, and ultimately no life, without community."
>
> – M. Scott Peck, psychiatrist

WRITE

Imagine the type of people who would make up your ideal community. Explore below what qualities they would embody. How would you spend your time together? Would you have similar views on the world? If they challenged your beliefs, how would you resolve those differences? Think about the spaces in your life where this imaginary network might exist.

The demographics of the people I am drawn to: _____

_____

_____

_____

The values and qualities that I seek out in others: _____

_____

_____

_____

> **Marginal Wisdom**
>
> "We are looking to brands for poetry and for spirituality, because we're not getting those things from our communities or from each other."
>
> – Naomi Klein, author

The world views or beliefs that I would want to have in common: _____

_____

_____

_____

The ways we would resolve a clash or differing of opinions: _____

_____

_____

_____

How I would feel, physically and emotionally, when we're together: _____

_____

_____

_____

EXPLORE

We live in a time of toxic polarization, where nearly everything has become politicized, and every topic can feel divisive. Climate change, history, medicine, gender, books, even light bulbs. In America, at least, it sometimes feels like any two citizens can have a completely different experience and point of view on what used to be given facts.

The truth is, neither "side" is right or wrong. Both have their benefits and deficits. But as author Arthur Brooks says, "We need to learn to disagree better." Community is easy when everyone is on the same page, but how do we bridge the giant cultural divide that rampant misinformation, a dysfunctional two-party system, and a disunified country has created? What does a "healthy" or "successful" community look like in a time of great division? How can spiritual tools help us discover shared values and precious points of unity around which we can build soulful, respectful, and intentional communities?

Marginal Wisdom

"Without community, there is no liberation... but community must not mean a shedding of our differences, nor the pathetic pretense that these differences do not exist."

– Audre Lorde, poet and professor

Section 13: Creating Community

REFLECT

Dr. Martin Seligman, the father of positive psychology, has said that one of the paths to flourishing comes from "using your strengths in service of others." Think about some of the skills or offerings you bring to the spaces you occupy. (This is no time to practice humility!)

Indeed, most thriving communities are only that way because people within them stepped into clear roles to make the group more effective. Sometimes, the fastest way to find where you best belong is to figure out where you are most needed. Are you a leader? Connector? Where do you "fit" in a community structure? Below are some common roles within communities. Read them through. Which ones resonate with you?

The Leader
The one who sees the big picture, who can articulate possibilities, who inspires others to dream

The Doer
The one who gets things done, who prefers action over discussion, who stays late to make things happen

The Advocate
The one who raises collective awareness, who shares compelling stories, who ensures all voices are heard

The Connector
The one who brings people together, who connects dots and builds bridges, who knows everyone

The Healer
The one who is empathic, who notices when people need help or support, who offers guidance

The Helper
The one who has no problem jumping in to get things done, who prefers to be behind the scenes, who is always reliable

The Maker
The one who loves to create or express themselves, who pulls people together around music or art, who contributes beauty

The Mentor
The one who holds wisdom, who offers guidance or perspective, who remembers all the traditions and experiences

The Engineer
The one who loves to construct, build, and rig, who loves numbers and data

Marginal Wisdom

"People who are truly strong lift others up. People who are truly powerful bring others together."

– Michelle Obama, former First Lady

Now, think through your specific skills and gifts—which role aligns most with what you offer? Which would you love to do . . . even if you were never asked? How do you naturally show up? Which drains you? Which fills you up? What do you bring that no one else does?

ACTIVITY

WARNING: DISCOMFORT AHEAD!

SPARKS WITH STRANGERS!

Every day this week, go to a public place (think a coffee shop, local park, college campus, or grocery store). Approach a stranger and strike up a conversation about something meaningful. Not the weather or just giving them a compliment (though that's always a nice way to start!). Instead, try to get to know something about this person. Look up from your phone and into their eyes. Make them feel seen. Log your conversations, and journal about how they made you feel below.

SUNDAY

Whom did you meet?	What did you talk about?	How did it go? What did you feel?

Marginal Wisdom

"My humanity is bound up in yours, for we can only be human together."

– Desmond Tutu, bishop and theologian

MONDAY

Whom did you meet?	What did you talk about?	How did it go? What did you feel?

TUESDAY

Whom did you meet?	What did you talk about?	How did it go? What did you feel?

WEDNESDAY

Whom did you meet?	What did you talk about?	How did it go? What did you feel?

THURSDAY

Whom did you meet?	What did you talk about?	How did it go? What did you feel?

FRIDAY

Whom did you meet?	What did you talk about?	How did it go? What did you feel?

SATURDAY

Whom did you meet?	What did you talk about?	How did it go? What did you feel?

ACTIVITY

CREATE A COMMUNITY ACTION PLAN!

*Choose a community where you feel a strong sense of belonging. It might be your family. It might be your church. It might just be an identity you care a lot about—"entrepreneur" or "proud local resident" or "teacher." List out **five** specific actions you can commit to today in order to be more engaged, supportive, or contributory to this community.*

The community I wish to better support or engage with is: _____

_____

_____

_____

Specific ways I can show up for this community right now:

- _____
  _____

- _____
  _____

- _____
  _____

- _____
  _____

- _____
  _____

TIME TO COMMIT!

Sign the statement below. Then, take a picture of this page and text it to a friend. Ask them to hold you accountable!

> **Marginal Wisdom**
>
> "There is no power for change greater than a community discovering what it cares about."
>
> – Margaret J. Wheatley, writer

I, _____, hereby commit to show up for this community. I will make every effort to take these actions now and into the future. I love what this community brings to my life, and I will support and strengthen my sense of belonging by engaging in the ways listed above.

Signed: _____

My Witness's Name: _____

Soul Boom Workbook: Spiritual Tools for Modern Living

ACTIVITY

JOIN IRL!

It's all well and good to think about community in our heads. But these days, it's easier and easier to cancel plans. To reschedule. To sign up but not show up.

Yet science tells us that our brains can travel quickly from obligation to enjoyment. Our prefrontal cortex kicks into gear when we feel responsible for showing up, but eventually, when we have a positive outcome (laughter, enjoying time with others), our brains flood with dopamine, and those obligations turn into positive, repeated habits.

In other words, consistently engaging in a community (even if it's out of a sense of duty) can often turn into an experience of genuine pleasure.

So let's get off those bums and get to work! Turn off the screens! It's time to join something IRL!

> **Marginal Wisdom**
>
> "Electric communication will never be a substitute for the face of someone who with their soul encourages another person to be brave and true."
>
> – Charles Dickens, author and novelist

STEP 1.
Make a list of all the activities, hobbies, and issues that you used to regularly do, find interesting, are curious about, or care about (e.g., playing the piano, black-and-white movies, EDM, kickball, knitting, role-playing games, immigration, etc.).

_____ _____
_____ _____
_____ _____
_____ _____
_____ _____

STEP 2.
Pick three of the activities you identified and start searching! Find a local group or organization and learn more about it. Check out your local city or junior college. Or go to a physical space. Think, "I'm interested in knitting; let me see if there are any clubs at my local crafts store."

STEP 3.
Now, pick one! Reach out by email, text, or DM and get information on how to sign up. Put the first three meetings or dates in your calendar. Pay the deposit for the class. Tell your mom or your best friend or your kids that you're doing it.

STEP 4.
Show up! That's it. That's the task.

REMEMBER!
Feeling belonging and enjoyment from this activity isn't something that will happen overnight. It takes time. So give yourself the gift of time and stick with it for at least two months. Your brain will thank us!

ACTIVITY

GATHER IN SPIRIT!

Your turn to organize something! And we want you to organize a ... wait for it ... spiritually inspired gathering! If this feels daunting, we get it. But we think it will pay off!

In The Art of Gathering, *sociologist Priya Parker says intentionality is the key to creating meaningful community. So consider what your ideal spiritual gathering would look like. Where would it be? What's the tone—playful, reverent? Who would you invite? Go back to pages 238-239 and remind yourself of the role you would best play in this gathering. Perhaps find some friends who might fill other roles and utilize all your strengths.*

Neuroscience tells us that oxytocin (the "bonding hormone") increases during mutual storytelling and shared rituals. So maybe start there. If you need some inspiration for other activities to gather around, here are a handful for you!

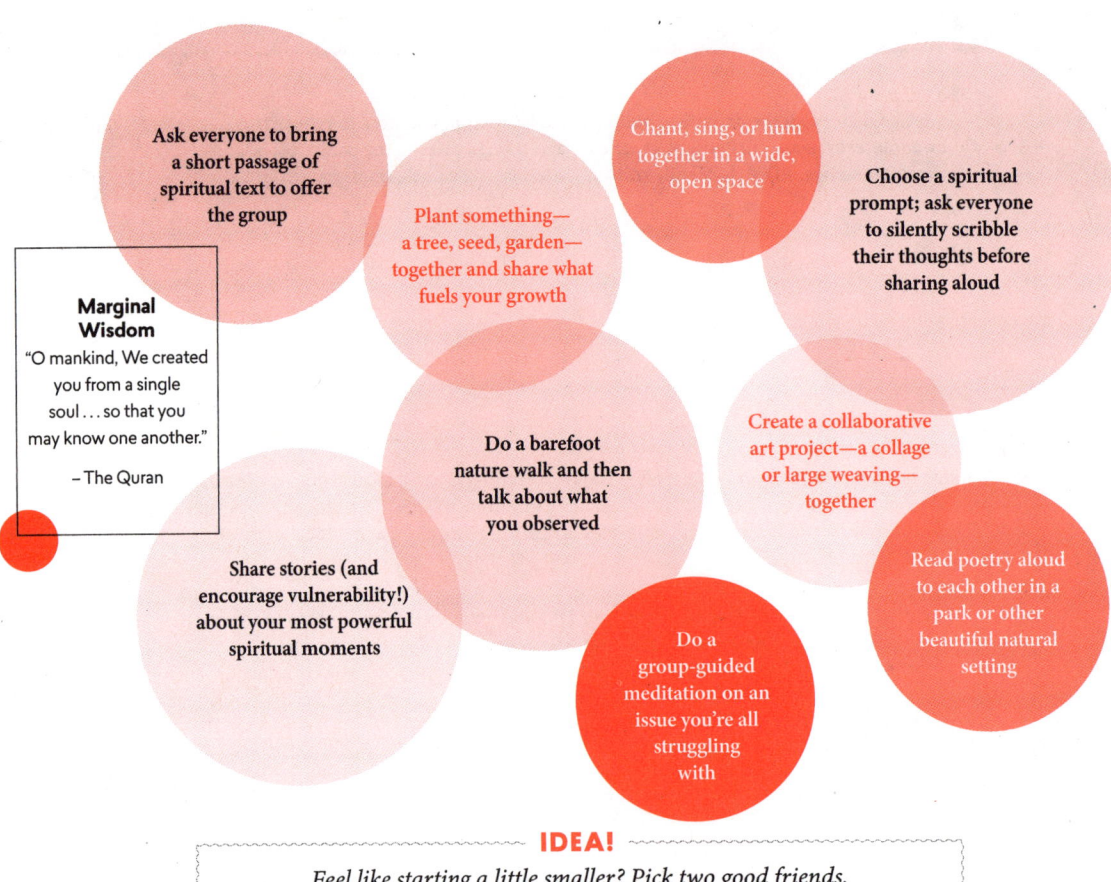

Marginal Wisdom
"O mankind, We created you from a single soul ... so that you may know one another."
– The Quran

- Ask everyone to bring a short passage of spiritual text to offer the group
- Plant something—a tree, seed, garden—together and share what fuels your growth
- Chant, sing, or hum together in a wide, open space
- Choose a spiritual prompt; ask everyone to silently scribble their thoughts before sharing aloud
- Do a barefoot nature walk and then talk about what you observed
- Create a collaborative art project—a collage or large weaving—together
- Share stories (and encourage vulnerability!) about your most powerful spiritual moments
- Do a group-guided meditation on an issue you're all struggling with
- Read poetry aloud to each other in a park or other beautiful natural setting

IDEA!
Feel like starting a little smaller? Pick two good friends. Make them coffee. And do an activity from this book together! Discuss what stirs your spirit and what spiritual connections you long for.

REFLECT

REMINDER: DON'T FORGET SELF-CARE!

We just spent a lot of time encouraging you to get out, engage with, commit to, and build community. That was a lot of work we just asked of you!

But the truth is, being actively in community can sometimes feel like a lot—group settings are extremely demanding of our personal time and energy and resources! So as we wrap up this section, we want to honor and acknowledge that it's OK to need quiet, stillness, and time to recharge. Feeling burned out by all that togetherness-work is real. And finding space for solitude—but not isolating—while still within a community is an art form. What are some ways you can recharge, rest, and manage feelings of overwhelm while you're engaged in community?

> **Marginal Wisdom**
> "Compassion for others begins with kindness to ourselves."
> – Pema Chodron, Tibetan Buddhist nun

Section 13: Creating Community

Section 14

A SERVICE MINDSET

THE world doesn't need any more billionaires. Or supermodels. Or flavors of Doritos. Today, what the world needs more than ever is people who seek to be useful. People who roll up their sleeves and ask, "How can I be of service today?"

Unfortunately, our society has service all mixed up. We often look admiringly at the people taking the big actions—writing a large check to a nonprofit or recruiting a hundred people to a beach cleanup.

At *Soul Boom*, we believe intentionally choosing to quietly serve others is a revolutionary act. True service means offering a couch to your friend going through a divorce, picking up trash on your morning walk, or emailing someone a job lead. And we believe cultivating a service mindset in all people has the power to transform the world—to radically usher in its spiritual healing and progress.

Across spiritual traditions, service work is sacred work. It's a path to God. In Christianity, Jesus washed the feet of his disciples, saying, "I have set you an example that you should do as I have done for you." The Buddha taught that serving others with compassion is a direct path to liberation from self. Across faiths and cultures, service helps to interweave our lives with others and reminds us that we're inexorably connected.

And bonus! Service is really good for us! A 2020 study published in *The Journal of Happiness Studies* found that people who volunteered regularly experienced lower levels of depression, greater life satisfaction, and longer lifespans. A Carnegie Mellon study showed that adults who volunteered 200 or more hours a year had lower blood pressure than those who didn't. Basically, serving others is figuratively—and literally!—good for the heart.

In a world overwhelmed by massive, complicated problems and conflicts, quiet acts of service can feel . . . small. But small is where the magic lives. People feel empowered and helpful—experiencing what researchers call "the helper's high"—when they take local, personal actions.

If this feels hard, we get it. It can sometimes seem like we need to have more—more skills, resources, access—in order to serve effectively. But as Martin Luther King Jr. once said: "Everybody can be great . . . because anybody can serve. You don't have to have a college degree to serve. You don't have to make your subject and verb agree to serve. You only need a heart full of grace. A soul generated by love."

So this section is about taking our "heart full of grace" and "soul generated by love" and cultivating a mind geared toward service alongside them. We will try to connect the dots between our small sparks of service and the flames of change.

Because when you serve, you don't just help others, you draw out the purest parts of your soul. You become useful. And that, maybe more than anything else, is what gives life meaning.

FIELD NOTES!

Spoiler Alert: The Meaning of Life Is Service
By Rainn Wilson

In order to find the meaning of life, I once journeyed to the roof of the world and met with a Tibetan monk.

No big deal.

On the edge of said roof of the world sits the Indian town of Dharamshala. It is one of the loveliest and most holy places I've ever visited—nestled against the wall of the Himalayan mountains, which stretch north hundreds of kilometers and contain 10 of the 14 peaks on Planet Earth that are more than 26,000 feet tall.

Himalaya means "abode of snow." And while snow is not something you think of when you think of the subcontinent of India, there was plenty of it up there, believe me. As well as 15,000 glaciers. (And lots and lots of cute and crazy monkeys!)

Dharamshala means "shelter of dharma" and is the mountain town where His Holiness the Dalai Lama has made his home since 1960. There are hundreds of monks who live in this "Little Tibet," and about 100,000 Tibetans living throughout India who escaped their homeland when the Chinese invaded in the 1950s.

My wife and I, along with some other fascinating folks (like Rich Roll and Arthur Brooks and the editor of *The Atlantic* magazine), got to have a group meeting with HHDL (His Holiness the Dalai Lama), and it was a beautiful experience and a tremendous honor. He spoke for about an hour on the power of love to change the world and the importance of always turning our attention to the cosmic force of love.

But the real treat? Meeting with a real-life Tibetan monk named Thabke, who had lived in a monastery since he was a child and had recently been studying meditation's effect on the brain at a university in southern India. I got to interview him on-camera for a very special episode of the *Soul Boom* podcast.

My main question for Thabke was a simple one. I said, "Imagine you're a holy man from a *New Yorker* cartoon, and you've been living your whole life in a cave in the mountains, meditating on the totality of existence. And pretend I had just spent weeks crawling up to meet with you, and as I made it to the entrance of your cave where you were sitting cross-legged, I asked on hands and knees, 'Oh, monk! Please answer me! What is the meaning of life?' What would your answer be?"

Thabke thought about this for a while and said, quite simply, with a radiant smile, "Service!"

He then started to break this idea down.

When you focus your life around service, this addresses the problems of the self-serving ego and gets one closer to the Buddhist idea of *anatta* or "no self."

Also? The people you end up serving benefit from your work.

And the kicker? The more one focuses on serving others and being "other-centered" instead of "self-centered," the happier and more whole one ultimately becomes!

This concept is a centerpiece of so many spiritual traditions and belief systems. The great mystic teacher Sri M said:

"When you serve a less fortunate person in any way, material or spiritual, you are not doing him a favor. In fact, he who receives your help does you a favor by accepting what you give, and thereby helps you to evolve and move closer to the Divine, Blissful Being who, in reality, is within you and in the hearts of all beings."

It feels counterintuitive, I know, but this idea has also been borne out by dozens of studies in positive psychology. In a 2008 study by the London School of Economics, people who volunteered monthly were 7% more likely to report being "very happy." For those who volunteered weekly, the number went up to 16%, similar to the happiness boost you get from doubling your income!

And yet on social media and in the popular imagination, we focus all of our time and energy on pursuing money and almost none on increasing service to others. The American Dream is centered on achieving material gain, not on following in the example of Jesus Christ to serve the poor and give of one's time.

This conversation has stayed with me ever since and forces me to wrestle with my daily choices. Am I truly doing enough? Could I be giving more in order to partake in this rich meal of life's essential meaning? Sure, I talk a good game, but am I truly engaged in some kind of daily service that uplifts others *AND* myself?

So you heard it here folks, straight from a Tibetan monk's mouth. Service to others is the cornerstone of the meaning of life. And guess what? We've got a whole section about this idea for you to dig around in.

Actually, now that I think of it, I have done you all a tremendous service by creating this chapter on service. I feel better already! See how that works? Enjoy. (And you're welcome!)

Marginal Wisdom

"The end of all knowledge should be service to others."

– Cesar Chavez, civil rights activist

DEFINE

Let's dig into what having "a service mindset" means to you. Does it always have to be selfless? Do you think service is more impactful when it's smaller or bigger? Why? What might it look like to live with the intention of being useful, and how might the world change if more of us made service our default modus operandis? To be "other-centered" rather than "self-centered"? Freewrite about your thoughts on service below.

> **Marginal Wisdom**
>
> "I slept and dreamt that life was joy. I awoke and saw that life was service. I acted, and behold, service was joy."
>
> – Rabindranath Tagore, poet, artist, and philosopher

Section 14: A Service Mindset

REFLECT

Think back on the past seven days. In a week's time, what service work did you engage in? Start with the personal—the small ways you support your family, show up for your friends, or care for pets and children. Did you fold the laundry at home? Make coffee for your boss without being asked? Pick up trash on your walk home from the subway?

Then, think about what you do to lift up or help the immediate communities you belong to. Did you organize the group text to plan a friend's surprise birthday? Do you play the piano in your temple every week? List out all the ways you already exhibit a spirit of service, even if you've never specifically called it that.

> **Marginal Wisdom**
>
> "It is the greatest of all mistakes to do nothing because you can only do little—do what you can."
>
> – Sydney Smith, Anglican cleric and writer

ACTIVITY

SERVICE WITH A SMILE!

Catholic nun and saint Mother Teresa once said, "Every time you smile at someone, it is an action of love, a gift to that person, a beautiful thing." Let's practice giving this powerful but inexpensive gift to others.

Stand by the door of a public place (think a gym or grocery store or, better yet, the DMV). Hold the door open for people entering. Greet them with a hello, good afternoon, and, most importantly, the most genuine SMILE you can offer. Do this for 10–15 minutes. Then, walk away. Journal about the experience and how it made you feel below.

> **Marginal Wisdom**
>
> "I love people who make me laugh. I honestly think it's the thing I like most—to laugh. It cures a multitude of ills. It's probably the most important thing in a person."
>
> – Audrey Hepburn, actress

WRITE

Researchers at Stanford University have found that acts of kindness toward others increase our well-being and can create a ripple effect of goodwill for others. Describe a time when someone's act of kindness made a significant impact on your life. How did this experience make you feel? Did it inspire you to undertake a similar action? What dominos did that act of kindness tip over in your life?

Marginal Wisdom

"No one is useless in this world who lightens the burdens of another."

– Charles Dickens, author

DRAW

Now, bring the answer to the previous question to life! Think about this memorable act of service that someone did for you. Below, draw the moment this person engaged in service toward you. Capture the event with rich visual imagination. Radiate their kindness with color and energy and how it impacted your heart. (Note: If you want to illustrate a different example than the one you wrote about on the previous page, go for it!)

> **Marginal Wisdom**
>
> "I cannot do all the good that the world needs, but the world needs all the good that I can do."
>
> – Jana Stanfield, gospel singer-songwriter

ACTIVITY

A LEGACY OF SERVICE!

In the ancient practice of Sufism, there is a strong emphasis placed on wisdom and learning through lived experiences. We love this idea! Maybe the best way to learn how to be of service is to talk to someone who embodies that way of being in the world. While we know many jobs can be seen as a form of service, we want you to find someone whose work centers on the care of others (e.g., a nurse, teacher, stay-at-home mom, nonprofit employee, pro bono lawyer). Complete this "Legacy of Service" interview with them to understand what sustains them.

MY INTERVIEW WITH _____

What do you do, and who do you do it for? _____

_____

What first inspired you to want to do work that cares for others?

_____

_____

_____

_____

What does "service" mean to you—not just the word but the feeling behind it? How would you describe it to someone who's never thought about it before?

_____

_____

_____

_____

What keeps you going when the work is hard, thankless, or emotionally exhausting?

_____

_____

_____

_____

Do you see your work as connected to anything spiritual, sacred, or deeply personal?
_____
_____
_____

What sacrifices have you made to do this work—and would you make them again?
_____
_____
_____

> **Marginal Wisdom**
>
> "Anyone who does anything to help a child in his life is a hero to me."
>
> – Fred Rogers, minister, author, and children's TV personality

Can you share a story of a time when your work really impacted someone? How did it make you feel?
_____
_____
_____
_____

What would you say to someone who feels they don't have enough time, money, or energy to be of service?
_____
_____
_____
_____

This last question is for YOU. What does this conversation tell you about what it takes to devote your life to serving others? How did hearing their thoughts make you feel? Reflect below.

ACTIVITY

APPRECIATE THE INVISIBLE!

All around you are people doing service work that goes unnoticed. The bus drivers, custodians, dishwashers, house cleaners, and caregivers in society. The individuals whose contributions often go overlooked in making the world, our neighborhoods, even our families run more smoothly. Write a letter of appreciation to someone doing invisible work near you—at home, at work, or in your community. Cultivate empathy and gratitude for their contributions. Honor their unseen acts of love and service. (You can either follow our prompts below or just freewrite from the heart!)

Dear _____,

I wanted to say thank you for your daily work that most people don't notice. I see how you:

_____

_____

Your efforts create meaningful impact in the lives of: _____

_____

_____

> **Marginal Wisdom**
>
> "One who gives charity in secret is greater than Moses."
>
> – from the Talmud of Judaism

I notice that you do your work with a beautiful spirit by always: _____

_____

_____

I will never forget when I saw you: _____

_____

_____

So today, I just want to say thank you and: _____

_____

_____

With heartfelt gratitude, _____

★ BONUS ★

Channel your courage and give the person your letter. Then, walk away knowing you listened to what was in your heart and shared it with them.

EXPLORE

Service is often most effective when our actions align with our values. And psychologists say that we are also more motivated to take action when it is in line with what we believe. Think about some of the overall virtues and values you prioritize in your life, and write about what acts of service would allow you to express or live out those values. If helpful, refer back to that unit of work in Section 7. We have provided a couple of examples.

Value I Prioritize	Possible Acts of Service to Embody This Value
Education	*To volunteer to guest lecture at a local underserved school*
Generosity	*To gift donuts every week to my office coworkers*

Marginal Wisdom

"Service to others is the rent you pay for your room here on earth."

– Muhammad Ali,
boxer and social activist

Section 14: A Service Mindset   259

ACTIVITY

WARNING: TIME TO DO SOME ACTUAL SERVICE WORK!

IT'S MICROSERVICE WEEK!

Islam teaches that even the smallest good deed matters—"removing something harmful from the road is charity." Shabnam's husband, Toufan, for example, stocks their car with trash bags, gloves, grabbers, and a portable handwashing station. All so he can quickly clean up any unsightly mess in their local parks, playgrounds, beaches, and walks for everyone to enjoy.

Every day this week, fill in this microservice ledger with the tiny, intentional things you do to be of service or useful to others. Let's go!

SUNDAY

My act of microservice:

How it made me feel:

MONDAY

My act of microservice:

How it made me feel:

TUESDAY

My act of microservice:

How it made me feel:

WEDNESDAY

My act of microservice:

How it made me feel:

THURSDAY

My act of microservice:

How it made me feel:

FRIDAY

My act of microservice:

How it made me feel:

SATURDAY

My act of microservice:

How it made me feel:

Marginal Wisdom

"Stay busy. Be useful."

– Arnold Schwarzenegger, actor and former governor

Section 14: A Service Mindset

ACTIVITY

MY INCONVENIENCE MAP!

Service work and giving can often be influenced by social norms (volunteering for college credit!), tax benefits, or public perception (billionaires signing the Giving Pledge so they aren't called out!). The truth is, there's nothing wrong with this type of giving or service work. It's still good for us and the world.

There is a better alternative, however. Altruistic giving involves no expectation of reward or recognition; it's driven by empathy or deep love; and most importantly, it often comes with an element of sacrifice—altruistic giving inconveniences you in some way. In other words, the more we "feel" our giving—the more it costs us in time, effort, or comfort—the more fulfilling it can be. According to a 2016 study in Emotion, giving that is "effortful" increases well-being and long-term satisfaction, and actions that require sacrifice are interpreted as more meaningful, both to the giver and receiver. It tells you (and others) that you deeply, authentically CARE.

We'll give you an example. When your friend asks for a ride to the airport at 5 a.m., it can be really tempting to schedule and pay for an Uber (guilty!) rather than wake up at 4:30 in the morning. But this act of inconvenient service is way better for our well-being.

So let's practice some self-reflection here and explore just how inconvenienced your service and giving efforts make you.

Below, list *five* instances where you've given something—time or money, energy, action, advice, care. Consider the giving you do regularly, as well as the giving that you haven't done in a while.

A _____
_____

B _____
_____

C _____
_____

D _____
_____

E _____
_____

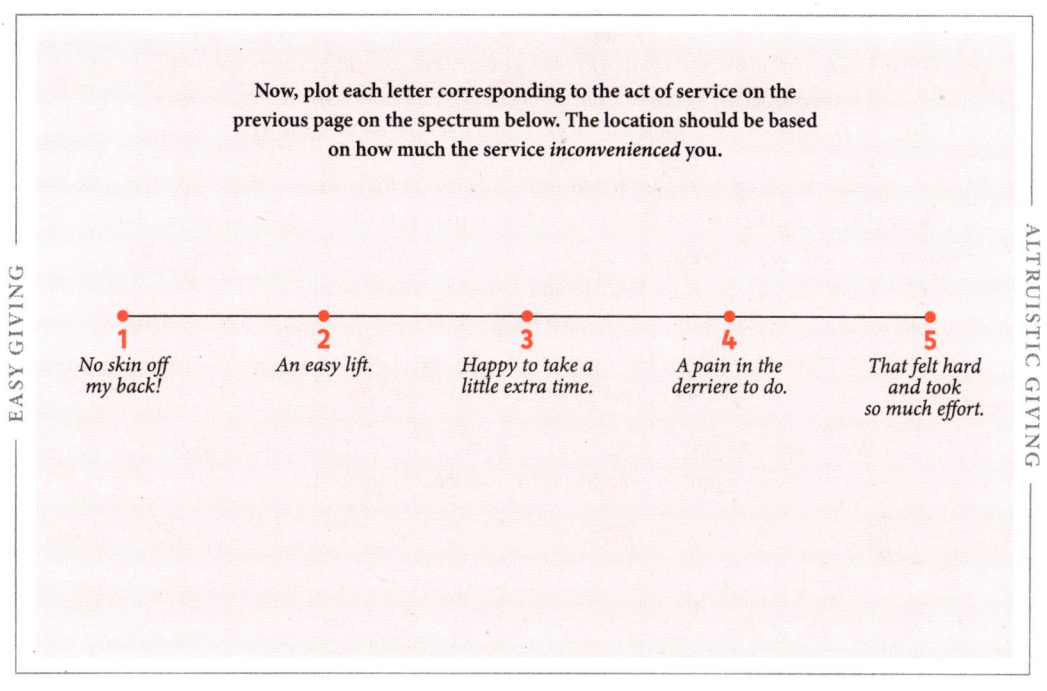

Time to reflect! Where does your giving tend to fall? What level of sacrifice do you feel comfortable making when you rise to serve or give? Why do you think that is? How would you define meaningful service in your life after working through this activity?

Marginal Wisdom

"Carry out a random act of kindness, with no expectation of reward, safe in the knowledge that one day, someone might do the same for you."

– Princess Diana, royal and humanitarian

Section 14: A Service Mindset   263

ACTIVITY

TAKE NOTICE!

Often, when we think about small ways to be of service, we default to what most would call "random acts of kindness." But let's consider for a moment: Is buying a cup of coffee for the person behind you or holding a door open for strangers too fleeting?

In many cases, noticing is the first step toward truly impactful service. Before action comes awareness. Research from the Making Caring Common Project at Harvard University shows that children who are taught to notice the needs of others—rather than simply being told what to do—are more likely to develop empathy, intuition, and initiative. Parents who regularly ask their kids, "What might this person need right now?" are encouraging their kids to adopt a habit of looking around, noticing what's missing, and answering that call for kindness, justice, or action.

Below, we're offering you eight ways to practice "noticing" and identifying needs that involve people in your local neighborhood.

Scan for gaps of care:
Where do you see people who seem isolated or neglected? Which bus stops or streets feel unsafe or ignored?

Listen to your intuition:
Do you ever think "someone should do something about that"? Could you be that person?

Observe natural spaces:
Who frequents the parks? What do they need? More trees, shade, or benches? A cleaner playground? For overflowing trash cans to be emptied?

Look with creative eyes:
What walls or alleys feel lifeless? Where would a mural or music or garden uplift the spirit of the people who live on a block?

Create a "mental map" of neighborhood neglect:
Have you noticed any ill or elderly neighbors? Which homes have signs of aging or overgrown gardens?

Check out your local NextDoor or Facebook group:
What posts are repeated? What are people often asking for? What offers for help have tons of engagement?

Ride public transportation:
Who is on the bus or train? What kinds of conversations are they having? What energy do you feel? Who is being overlooked?

Linger at a store checkout:
What are people buying—or not? Which families are struggling to find healthy foods?

Try practicing a few of these "noticing" exercises over the next week. Below, write about what you discover as neighborhood needs or opportunities for service. Think about what you saw and how you can help. What small acts of service can you undertake that would make an impact around you?

> **Marginal Wisdom**
>
> "Give your hands to serve, and your hearts to love."
>
> – Mother Teresa, Catholic nun and saint

Section 15

HOW
to
CHANGE
the
WORLD

WHEN *Soul Boom* launched, its mission was simple: to build the case for a spiritual revolution.

This workbook argues that the spiritual revolution will work only if it is twofold—both personal and social. Personal transformation is one thing, but creating spiritually inspired social change is . . . daunting. It requires action. It's complicated and sometimes messy. And slow.

Yet if you consider some of the major world changers of the past century—Mahatma Gandhi, Thich Nhat Hahn, Martin Luther King Jr., Malcolm X, Dorothy Day, Nelson Mandela, Helen Prejean—all of them grounded their movements in something deeper than political strategy. They pulled from faith, prayer, and scripture.

Gandhi read the Bhagavad Gita daily. His nonviolent approach to achieving independence for India was grounded in the sacred. "In the attitude of silence, the soul finds the path in a clearer light," he wrote. Nonviolence and Buddhist mindfulness were key to Thich Nhat Hahn's peaceful protests in opposition to the Vietnam War. MLK was a Baptist preacher first and a civil rights activist second. His protests for racial equity echoed like sermons. "Injustice anywhere is a threat to justice everywhere," he said.

Malcolm X began preaching unity across races after being transformed by his pilgrimage to Mecca. Workers' rights activist Day cofounded the Catholic Worker Movement because she believed serving the poor was a spiritual obligation. Mandela credited much of his approach to forgiveness—and reparations—to both traditional African and Christian theologies. Death row abolitionist Prejean was a Catholic nun moved by her faith to advocate for mercy, even for death row inmates.

Our modern approach to building a better world is littered with "social impact campaigns" and "calls to action" and GoFundMe fundraisers. We agree that these are effective tools for change. But people tend to back away slowly the minute you start talking about the spiritual inner work needed to both propel and sustain social change.

From our POV, meaningful change requires exuding love! Compassion! Justice! Peace! Mercy! All the foundational virtues that spiritual wisdom offers. In fact, very little lasting social impact has ever happened without someone daring to mix spiritual ideals (even if they aren't called that) with the powers of change.

A spiritual revolution needs people who can speak truth to power and yet be well-wishers of their oppressors. Who can act tactically but lead spiritually. Who understand that justice is both a policy goal and a spiritual bedrock.

Because here's the hardest truth of all: The work of trying to change the world will break your heart . . . while it also breaks it wide open. There will be setbacks. The march of progress will be slow and painful. And sometimes, the losses and injustices will feel overwhelming. Without spiritual tools like prayer, purpose, gratitude, and stillness, the champions of a better world will simply burn out.

So this section isn't just about changing the world. It's about doing it differently. We don't need more rage baiters or enlightenment gurus. We need people who will choose to quietly bestow compassion where they see it needed because they witness the presence of a soul/holy essence inside every human. In the words of the poet Jackie Hill Perry, "Something revolutionary happens in the heart when you recognize that every single person you will ever meet is made in the image of God."

Let's invite this revolution deep into our hearts and souls so that our deeds can follow. Because if you don't believe in something bigger, you might forget why changing the world mattered in the first place.

FIELD NOTES!

A Snowball Called Hopelessness
By Rainn Wilson

Toward the last moments of the amazing "Classy Christmas" episode of *The Office*, Dwight Schrute (my character) says to the camera, "In the end, the greatest snowball isn't a snowball at all. It's fear." It's an episode where Dwight is tormenting his nemesis Jim with the threat of a snowball fight to such a degree that being attacked with snowballs starts to haunt Jim, and he spirals toward a total meltdown.

I'll come back to this quote later because I want to reveal my own version of that classic, oft-quoted line.

I give a lot of speeches on college campuses about mental health struggles and spiritual revolutions, as well as funny stories from *The Office*. Over the years, one question has consistently risen to the top. I'll never forget the young woman in a floppy hat who raised her hand at Binghamton University in New York and asked, "Do you really think humanity can ever be anything other than cruel, greedy, and self-serving? Shouldn't we just figure out how to live with the reality that we're all kind of screwed?" Something to that effect.

In the mothership book, *Soul Boom: Why We Need a Spiritual Revolution*, I spoke a great deal about world peace—how it's something that so many aspired to in the '60s and '70s: beauty contestants, hippies, theologians, politicians. Even *Star Trek*. There were songs about it. Poems. Rallies with tens of thousands of people. As the specter of the Cold War and a possible nuclear winter hung over humanity, the longing for peace was tangible and urgent. If we're to have a spiritual revolution, we need to consider where we want to be headed, don't you think? What the end game is. Isn't it strange and sad that no one discusses world peace anymore? It's not even close to being on the greater human agenda.

As I began writing the original book during the pandemic, I also spoke about a plethora of *other* pandemics affecting humanity—racism, materialism, nationalism, mental health, income inequality. The list goes on. And on. And leads us to the granddaddy of them all, climate change.

It was Shabnam who directed me in *Soul Boom* to the idea of "hopepunk" as a genre of literature and storytelling that ran contrary to "grimdark" and other types of dystopian, apocalyptic stories that make up so much of the world of fantasy and science fiction. You can't turn on a television these days without a *The Last of Us*, *Squid Game*, or *The Handmaid's Tale* showing us how grotesque and futile the future is going to be.

I'm not saying all this to depress you, I promise. It's just that these various points, as well as the question the young woman with the floppy hat asked, led me toward a finding that is truly revelatory. Something that I missed in the mothership book.

And that is this: There is a pandemic that's far greater than all the ones I listed above. A problem even grander than the fact that we no longer discuss world peace or that our planet and species are plagued with various pandemics and our media is saturated with stories of impossibly dark and dystopian futures.

I've come to realize that the greatest pandemic of all is a lack of *hope*. The greatest threat to the future of humanity is that young humans are pessimistic that *change is even possible*. I mean, if you can't visualize anything positive on the horizon and lack any breeze of hope to help you on your journey, how does any kind of social transformation take place?

This is the insidious social cancer that all of us must fight. In the trenches of middle school, high school, and college campuses. In the whirligig mayhem of social media. In our homes with our children and at our workplaces. And especially in the battleground of our very own hearts.

That's where it hits heaviest for me. And the girl in the floppy hat in Binghamton. And for so many young people I hear from. But in order to have any kind of spiritual revolution, we have to first tackle this debilitating illness of cynicism and hopelessness.

My charge to you? Keep hope alive!

Ultimately, we must believe that humanity is as capable of change, growth, and transformative wisdom as it is of being selfish, cruel, and destructive. The greatest act of rebellion you can undertake is to inspire, uplift, and offer hope. Spread love and joy, gather and serve, give generously. Do it with kindness, prayer, and compassion. With a song on your lips. These are the battle cries and Trojan horses that will triumph over the rapidly deploying forces of lethargy, apathy, and despair.

So what is my personal version of that epic Dwight quote I opened with? It goes something like this: "In the end, the greatest pandemic isn't a pandemic at all. It's hopelessness."

Then, I would add, "And we can beat it. Don't be an idiot."

> **Marginal Wisdom**
>
> "We are called to assist the Earth to heal her wounds and, in the process, heal our own."
>
> – Wangari Maathai, environmental activist and Nobel laureate

REFLECT

In Soul Boom: Why We Need a Spiritual Revolution, Rainn outlined a "plethora of pandemics" affecting the world today. We've listed them below. Are there any others you would add? Fill in all that come to mind.

- Deaths of Despair (addiction, suicide)
- Racism
- Sexism
- Materialism
- Nationalism and Militarism

- Climate Change
- Other: _____
- Other: _____
- Other: _____
- Other: _____

Now, consider which of these pandemics directly affects your life. Which ones impact your neighborhood? Which have shown up in your country? Dig into how your life, family, and community have been personally touched by these systemic problems.

_____
_____
_____
_____
_____
_____
_____
_____
_____
_____
_____
_____
_____
_____
_____
_____
_____

> **Marginal Wisdom**
>
> "Not everything that is faced can be changed, but nothing can be changed until it is faced."
>
> – James Baldwin, writer and civil rights activist

EXPLORE

The Soul Boom POV argues that the root of the complex social, emotional, economic, and political problems listed and described in the last prompt are actually "spiritual in nature." What do you think might be at the root of the world's diseases? What spiritual shortcomings or deficits may be the cause of these societal ills? How might spirituality be used to heal those diseases? For example, could the root cancer causing racism be the "othering" of people instead of seeing all as members of one human family? Explore how a lack of soul wisdom may have led to the problems of this world—and how spirituality may also be the source of the solutions.

> **Marginal Wisdom**
>
> "An individual has not started living until he can rise above the narrow confines of his individualistic concerns to the broader concerns of all humanity."
>
> – Martin Luther King Jr., Baptist minister and civil rights activist

ACTIVITY

LISTEN TO YOUR HEARTBREAK!

Activist and Nobel Peace Prize winner Kailash Satyarthi has said that anyone with a conscience is an activist, but it's up to each of us to discover the issues that awaken our "inner activist." Spirituality author Parker Palmer urges people to engage in "listening to your heartbreak as guidance." So let's do that!

What's breaking your heart these days? Think of a recent news story or social issue that stirs strong emotion in you—grief, anger, urgency. What is awakening your inner activist? Write about this heartbreak, and what it stirs in you, below.

The issue / story / suffering that is breaking my heart these days is: _____

_____

Why does this issue matter to me? _____

> **Marginal Wisdom**
>
> "My faith is what gives me the courage to stand when it would be easier to sit down, to speak when silence feels safer."
>
> – Bryan Stevenson, lawyer and civil rights activist

What personal story or value does this issue tap into for me? _____

What is this heartbreak guiding me to want to do? _____

What action is my "inner activist" compelled to take to heal this heartbreak? _____

Section 15: How to Change the World

ACTIVITY

A BETTER WORLD VISION!

So you want to change the world? Cool! Let's start by putting on our big old imagination goggles and envisioning it first. It's hard to look around at Earth today and have any hope that things can be better. But hope is a funny thing—it's an unlimited resource. We just have to cultivate it. So let's start by filling in this worksheet—a worksheet for dreamers, doers, and troublemakers alike—that allows us to picture what a better world just might look like.

WHAT DOES IT *ACTUALLY* MEAN TO BUILD A BETTER WORLD?

Let's do a gut check! Select your instinctive reaction(s) when you hear someone say, "Let's build a better world!"

☐ Cringe and eye roll.

☐ Can I stick with my inner world, please?

☐ That sounds overwhelming. Does recycling count?

☐ Define "better." The world's not so bad.

☐ Heck yeah. Where's my tool kit?

☐ Is this a group project? I suck at group projects.

Which of these ideas would fit into your vision of a better world? Then, fill in a bunch more! A better world would be one where:

☐ No one sleeps outside unless they want to.

☐ Food is fresh, healthy, and freely shared.

☐ Mental health care is as normal as brushing your teeth.

☐ Mothers and motherhood are as revered as heads of state.

☐ Kids learn empathy and meditation before algebra.

☐ Access to clean water and clean air are God-given rights.

☐ Beauty is valued more than productivity.

☐ The natural world is protected like nuclear codes.

☐ Differences delight us, not divide us.

☐ Peace and justice replace greed and wealth.

☐ "I don't know" is seen as wisdom, not weakness.

☐ Joy and laughter and play are must-haves.

☐ Art is funded like the military, and murals are everywhere.

☐ Elders are revered mentors, not forgotten in retirement communities.

☐ Shame is replaced with accountability.

☐ Conflict is resolved with consultation, not violence.

☐ Other: _____

☐ Other: _____

☐ Other: _____

☐ Other: _____

Pick three words you would want to guide you in your contributions to creating a "better world."

☐ Connection   ☐ Love   ☐ Humility
☐ Community   ☐ Compassion   ☐ Selflessness
☐ Curiosity   ☐ Altruism   ☐ Trouble (the good kind)
☐ Courage   ☐ Gratitude   ☐ Other: _____
☐ Creativity   ☐ Calm   ☐ Other: _____

Now, fill in the blanks with the first things that come to mind when you think of building a "better world."

A better world is one where people _____
instead of _____.

A better world looks _____
_____.

A better world feels _____
_____.

I wonder what would happen if everyone just _____
_____.

I want to live in a world where _____
_____.

I am showing up to this work armed with _____
_____.

What are your takeaways? What ideas, values, and principles rose to the top for you? What do you think "better" means?

_____
_____
_____
_____
_____
_____
_____

> **Marginal Wisdom**
>
> "The great thing in the world is not so much where we stand as in what direction we are moving."
>
> – Oliver Wendell Holmes, poet

ACTIVITY

METTA KARUNA MUDITA!

The 13th-century Persian poet Rumi once wrote, "Yesterday I was clever, so I wanted to change the world. Today I am wise, so I am changing myself." We love the idea that changing the world starts with personal transformation. In Buddhism, that transformation happens by focusing on elevating our emotional state and capacity through three meditative practices that build on one another—loving-kindness (metta), compassion (karuna), and appreciative joy (mudita). Buddhist monk and peace activist Thich Nhat Hanh describes the relationship as so: "Loving-kindness overcomes hatred. Compassion overcomes cruelty. Appreciative joy overcomes envy. When these three practices are combined, a state of serenity is eventually attained called equanimity."

Let's think of some examples of how these principles could be applied IRL. Fill in this chart and imagine ways to put these spiritual principles to practical use.

Loving-Kindness overcomes **hatred**.	Describe a hatred you've witnessed, experienced, or read about:	What acts of loving-kindness might overcome this?
Compassion overcomes **cruelty**.	Describe a cruelty you've witnessed, experienced, or read about:	What acts of compassion might overcome this?
Appreciative Joy overcomes **envy**.	Describe an envy you've witnessed, experienced, or read about:	What acts of appreciative joy might overcome this?

Marginal Wisdom
"True spirituality is a revolutionary act.
It transforms the world by transforming ourselves."

– Marianne Williamson, author

EXPLORE

The Potential Project, a global leadership development and research organization, published a study in the Harvard Business Review in 2021 looking at how our understanding of someone else's experience affects our willingness to take action. Below is the spectrum of emotion and action they designed.

Study the graphic, and on the next pages, let's practice exercising these emotional muscles.

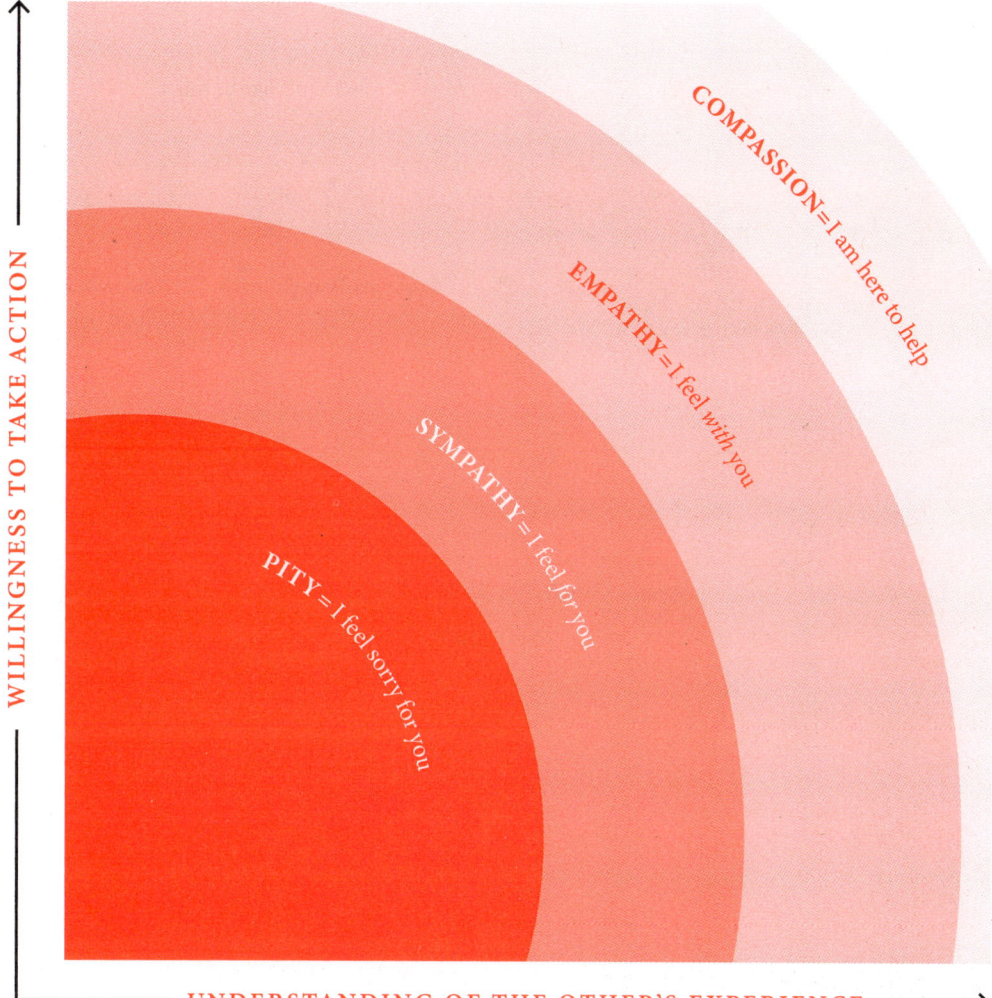

Section 15: How to Change the World

Think of an individual who is suffering or an issue you are passionate about. This might be someone you personally know or something you noticed from your work on pages 264-265. Write a statement exploring what each emotion might lead you to say and do. We've included an example.

THE ISSUE I NOTICED

A homeless mother and her two children panhandling on the street.

If I respond with:	
Pity "Poor things. What an awful way for children to grow up." *Do nothing.*	***Empathy*** "I feel her sadness. I know what it's like to suffer." *Buy the family a meal.*
Sympathy "She has it so hard, having to care for her kids in that situation." *Smile and give them $2.*	***Compassion*** "These souls are hurting. No child should live like that. I need to do something." *Call a local women's shelter and secure housing for them. Or join its board to help long term.*

THE ISSUE I NOTICED

_____

_____

If I respond with:	
Pity	***Empathy***
Sympathy	***Compassion***

THE ISSUE I NOTICED

_____
_____

If I respond with:	
Pity	*Empathy*
Sympathy	*Compassion*

Now, reflect on this exercise. If compassion is the ultimate source of willingness to take action to support someone, how can you cultivate more of it in your words, thoughts, and deeds?

_____
_____
_____
_____
_____
_____
_____
_____
_____
_____
_____
_____

> **Marginal Wisdom**
>
> "Hope is not about proving anything. It's about choosing to believe this one thing, that love is bigger than any grim, bleak [stuff] anyone can throw at us."
>
> – Anne Lamott, author

REFLECT

Here are 10 quotes about justice, compassion, and social action from a variety of spiritual, religious, and faith traditions. Read through them and see which resonates most with you.

"This is the sum of duty: do not do to others what would cause pain if done to you."

—Mahabharata 5:1517, Hinduism

"If you have come to help me, you are wasting your time. But if you have come because your liberation is bound up with mine, then let us work together."

—Murri proverb, Australian Aboriginal

"Right conduct is the supreme religion."

—Tattvartha Sutra 1.1, Jainism

"As a mother would protect her only child with her life, even so let one cultivate a boundless love toward all beings."

—Sutta Nipata 1.8, Buddhism

"There can be no doubt whatsoever that if the daystar of justice, which the clouds of tyranny have obscured, were to shed its light upon men, the face of the earth would be completely transformed."

—The Hidden Words, Baha'i Faith

"Learn to do good; seek justice, correct oppression; bring justice to the fatherless, plead the widow's cause."

—Isaiah 1:17, Judaism

"No one is my enemy, and no one is a stranger. I get along with everyone."

—Guru Granth Sahib 1299, Sikhism

"Do not impose on others what you do not wish for yourself."

—Analects 15:23, Confucianism

"None of you truly believes until he wishes for his brother what he wishes for himself."

—Sahih al-Bukhari, Islam

"He has sent me to proclaim freedom for the prisoners . . . to set the oppressed free, to proclaim the year of the Lord's favor."

—Luke 4:18–19, Christianity

280 *Soul Boom Workbook: Spiritual Tools for Modern Living*

Now, circle the ONE quote that feels like it resonates most with you. If this quote became the compass for all your choices and actions when engaging with the world, how would you behave differently? If you were faced with a crisis or injustice, how would your highest self, as shaped by this ancient wisdom, respond? What would you prioritize?

> **Marginal Wisdom**
>
> "Be willing to be a beginner every single morning."
>
> – Meister Eckhart, Catholic mystic and theologian

EXPLORE

When the news alerts start pummeling our phones in the morning, it can feel overwhelming. Injustice. Conflict. Greed. War. It feels impossible to address these global conflicts that exist at a macrolevel. But what if you could have a microresponse in your own life to a major conflict? Below is a list of several dozen major macrolevel conflicts, issues, and crises facing humanity at a global level.

Warning: This is pretty much guaranteed to make you depressed. But don't let that stop you!

- ☐ Climate change
- ☐ Species extinction
- ☐ Deforestation
- ☐ Water scarcity
- ☐ Poor air quality
- ☐ Plastic pollution
- ☐ Soil erosion and agricultural collapse
- ☐ War and military conflict
- ☐ Nuclear proliferation
- ☐ Terrorism and extremist violence
- ☐ Ethnic cleansing and genocides
- ☐ Refugee crises
- ☐ Rise of authoritarianism
- ☐ Decline of democratic institutions
- ☐ Political corruption
- ☐ Voter disenfranchisement
- ☐ Ineffective global governing institutions
- ☐ Nationalism and xenophobia
- ☐ Political polarization
- ☐ Extreme wealth inequality
- ☐ Poverty and lack of access to basic needs
- ☐ Unemployment and underemployment
- ☐ Materialism and rampant consumerism
- ☐ Global debt crisis
- ☐ Unregulated tech monopolies
- ☐ Global pandemics
- ☐ Unequal access to healthcare
- ☐ Mental health crises
- ☐ Declining maternal healthcare
- ☐ Declining support for the family unit
- ☐ Lack of protection for childhood
- ☐ Rise in chronic diseases
- ☐ Malnutrition and food insecurity
- ☐ Lack of clean water and sanitation
- ☐ Aging populations
- ☐ Drug addiction and overdose epidemics
- ☐ Health misinformation
- ☐ Lack of public health infrastructure
- ☐ Artificial intelligence
- ☐ Tech addiction and digital dependency
- ☐ Loss of privacy
- ☐ Unregulated biotech and gene editing
- ☐ Global education inequality
- ☐ Attacks on journalists and press freedom
- ☐ Political propaganda and culture wars
- ☐ Loss of Indigenous knowledge
- ☐ Lack of moral or ethical education
- ☐ Loss of meaning and purpose
- ☐ Widespread loneliness and isolation
- ☐ Collective despair

Now, choose **three** of these major macrolevel conflicts. How can you address these conflicts by "thinking globally and acting locally"? What would it look like to have a microresponse at home, at work, or in your neighborhood? For example, if journalistic freedom is what you value, could you volunteer for ProPublica? If you care about clean water, is there a local environmental group you can join? Consider this as you work through your responses below.

The macrolevel issue: _____

My microresponse: _____

The macrolevel issue: _____

My microresponse: _____

> **Marginal Wisdom**
>
> "I will not allow my life's light to be determined by the darkness around me."
>
> – Sojourner Truth, former slave and abolitionist

The macrolevel issue: _____

My microresponse: _____

EXPLORE

Soul Boom *argues that it is easier to protest something than to build something. Do you agree? Take some time to intentionally investigate and engage with what is being BUILT to solve and address the inequities and challenges in the world. Search the Nice News or Reasons to Be Cheerful archives. Ask Google or ChatGPT for suggestions. Then write about **five** such solutions or stories that give you hope below.*

1.

2.

3.

4.

5.

EXPLORE

Use this space to freewrite about a time in your own life when you witnessed your community, neighborhood, city, or state come together. Where have you found moments of beauty or strength or interesting solutions during a crisis? Explore all the good you've personally witnessed being built.

> **Marginal Wisdom**
>
> "Start where you are. Use what you have. Do what you can."
>
> – Arthur Ashe, tennis champion

EXPLORE

Talking about changing the world feels ... daunting. We get it. And a cynical person might say, "What's the point anyway?" No one person is going to solve, say, racism. Picking up one piece of trash won't put a dent in climate change. Sadly, that's true. The Malala Yousafzais and José Andréses of the world are, indeed, rare. It is possible to spend a lifetime trying to build a better world but not living to see that world come to life; you're truly playing the long game. In that way, justice, peace, and change are often seen as a multigenerational effort. The seeds you plant now could become trees whose shade you never sit under.

How does this idea make you feel? Why might it be important to work for a better world, even if you don't live to see its progress? How can you keep feelings of cynicism or the disappointment of setbacks at bay?

> **Marginal Wisdom**
>
> "You can never leave footprints that last if you are always walking on tiptoe."
>
> – Leymah Gbowee, peace activist

ACTIVITY

SPIRITUAL SPEECHWRITER!

Imagine you are the speechwriter for an influential head of state. Or that you're about to give a commencement speech to 5,000 graduating college students. Write an inspiring two- to three-minute speech about why compassion for others—and the world—matters. Infuse your words with all the spiritual wisdom you've acquired. Use humor, stories, and data to compel the audience to care about the issues that you care about. (And please don't rely on AI. We want to hear YOUR voice!)

> **Marginal Wisdom**
>
> "Change will not come if we wait for some other person or some other time. We are the ones we've been waiting for. We are the change that we seek."
>
> – Barack Obama, US president

★ BONUS ★

What's preventing you from sharing these ideas now? Consider submitting your speech to the opinion column of a local newspaper. Post your insights and use the hashtag #SoulBoom. Better yet, start your own blog or newsletter or social media account! Share your thoughts regularly and freely with a broader audience. Your voice matters, too!

ACTIVITY

TOOLS FOR TURBULENT TIMES!

One of the most challenging parts of the hard, slow work of changing the world is what to do when you hit a wall. How do you replenish yourself when you're feeling tired or drained or hopeless? We believe spirituality offers the solutions to that as well!

Below is a cheat sheet of spiritual tools that can give you sustenance in turbulent times. It is a refresher on the many spiritual and philosophical practices we have already explored in this book that bear repeating in order to help you stay grounded, even when it all feels like too much.

CONSCIOUS BREATHING

When to use it
When you're feeling overwhelmed or anxious

Why it works
Intentional breath work can regulate the nervous system and return your awareness to the "now."

GRATITUDE PRACTICE

When to use it
When your world feels overly pessimistic

Why it works
Acknowledging what is good in your life helps your brain counteract its natural negativity bias and builds resilience.

DO AN ACT OF KINDNESS

When to use it
When you're deep in self-doubt

Why it works
Even the smallest acts of service shift your energy from rumination to agency—and connect you to others.

MEDITATE

When to use it
When your mind feels loud and rushed

Why it works
Moments of stillness and reflection can help you differentiate between thoughts and truth and generate clarity.

MOVEMENT

When to use it
When you're feeling stuck "in your head"

Why it works
Walking, exercise, dance, and yoga can all help purge emotions out of your body.

VISION BOARD

When to use it
When everything feels like a dumpster fire

Why it works
Imagining the world you want to build can remind you that all change starts with simple ideas.

TAKE A SACRED PAUSE (OR DO A SCREEN DETOX)

When to use it
When you're feeling tired or burned out

Why it works
A regular practice of resetting is its own form of resistance that can help renew your resolve for action.

GATHER WITH A COMMUNITY

When to use it
When you're feeling isolated or invisible

Why it works
Sitting in community reminds you there are others to carry your burdens and can help you feel seen.

PRAY OR READ SACRED TEXTS

When to use it
When you're feeling lost or without purpose

Why it works
Grounding words can anchor you in wisdom and remind you that others have kept going, too.

Now, take some time to think about a real emotional struggle you are dealing with lately in the work of bettering the world. Write about how you've been feeling. Explore which of the tools above might help you navigate that pain with more grace, composure, and insight. Freewrite your thoughts below.

> **Marginal Wisdom**
>
> "If you get tired, learn to rest, not to quit."
>
> – Banksy, street artist and activist

ACTIVITY

SOUL BOOM MAD LIBS!

Fill in this Mad Libs-style sheet to create a commitment plan for what it means to apply your new spiritual POV in the world. Think of this as your personalized plan for living a life filled with spiritually inspired actions.

MY SPIRITUALITY IN ACTION PLAN: A MAD LIBS GAME!

I, _____ (your name), commit to unleash my spirituality into the world. I believe that the world needs more _____ (positive behavior, value, or virtue). And the world needs a lot less _____ (harmful behavior or vice). My spiritual journey has taught me that I am here not just to exist but to _____ (spiritually inspired verb, such as "heal" or "create" or "serve"). I feel most spiritually alive when I am _____ (activity or space, such as "in nature" or "meditating").

And I practice my spiritual values regularly by _____ (spiritual ritual or habit). One challenge in the world that breaks my heart is _____ (issue, injustice, or -ism). I believe that I can slowly begin to help by _____ (small, specific action). The gifts I bring are _____ (personal qualities or skills).

I commit to using my gifts to specifically support _____ (group, cause, or person). I will hold myself accountable to this work via _____ (structure, process, or support system). And when things get tough, I will ground myself by thinking about _____ (a core belief, idea, image, or quote).

Because I believe that _____ (inspiring statement, such as "love is all you need"). May my commitment find all the _____ (resources or type of support) it needs to come to life.

Marginal Wisdom

"Every great dream begins with a dreamer. Always remember, you have within you the strength, the patience, and the passion to reach for the stars to change the world."

– Harriet Tubman, abolitionist and activist

Soul Boom Workbook: Spiritual Tools for Modern Living

WRITE

This is it! Your last official prompt of this spiritual journey. We've spent many of the past few pages focused on activities and action plans and the "doing" work of changing the world. But at Soul Boom, we believe what you plant in spirit grows in deeds!

On this final page, plant in spirit the change you want to see in the world. Consider Mother Teresa's admonition: "The problem with the world is that we draw the circle of our family too small." So draw the circle of your words wide and write a personal prayer, poem, blessing, or intention that includes the entire planet that we live on and the interconnected human family that occupies it. You can be poetic, mystical, funny, and/or heartfelt. Ready, go!

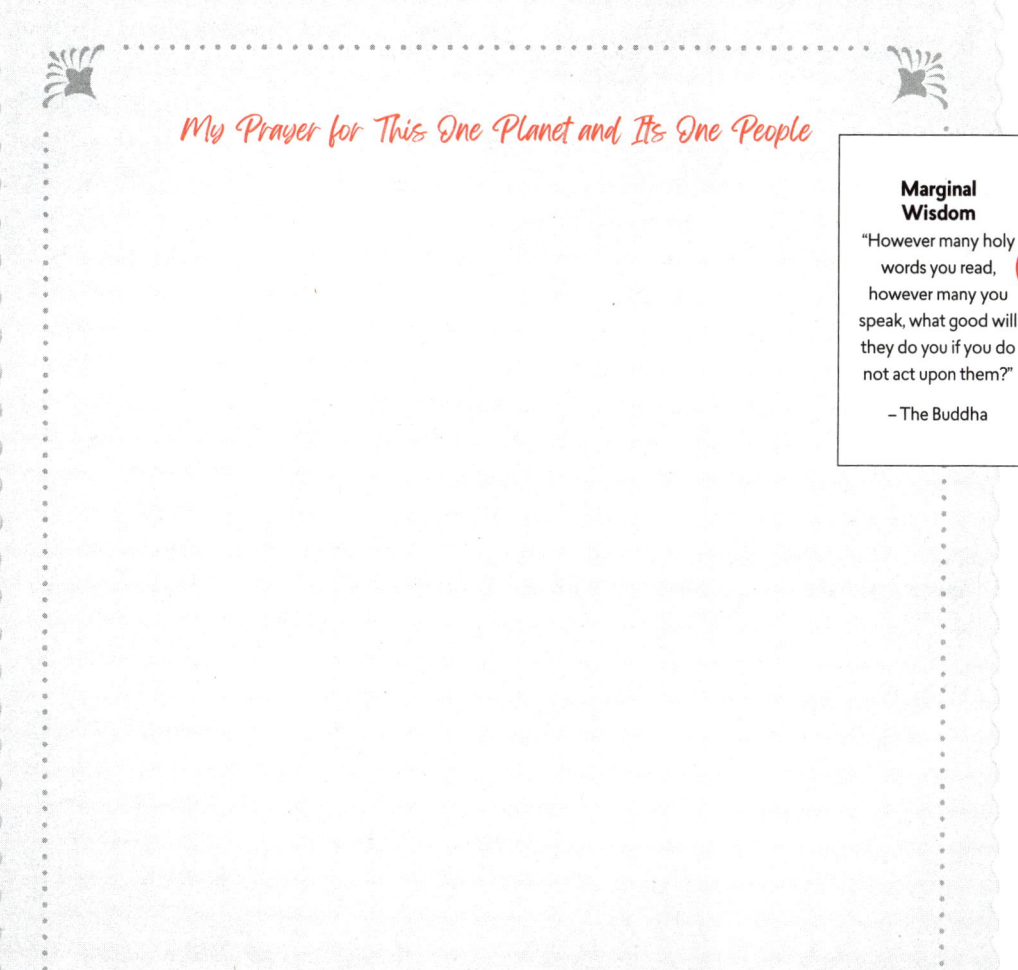

My Prayer for This One Planet and Its One People

Marginal Wisdom

"However many holy words you read, however many you speak, what good will they do you if you do not act upon them?"

– The Buddha

Section 15: *How to Change the World*

PAUSE & PONDER

You've done the personal, internal work; you've wrestled with the hard stuff; and now you've experimented with ways to put spiritual ideas into action in your daily life. This section of work on applying spirituality in our modern lives to create a better world could have been its own workbook. We weren't able to dig into every single issue, disease, and crisis the world faces and what kinds of spiritual wisdom could be applied. But we hope we have offered you a framework for thinking about what a spiritual revolution to make a better world could look and feel like.

Take a minute to flip back through the pages of Part Four. Reflect on your journey thus far below.

What was your favorite writing prompt, reflection, or activity? Why? What did it reveal about yourself?	**Which prompt, reflection, or activity was the most challenging for you or made you the most uncomfortable? Why do you think that is?**
As you wrap up these pages, which explore how spirituality can create a better world, what are your biggest takeaways from this unit of work?	**Draw, doodle, or sketch any final images that pop into your head as you move forward on your spiritual journey.**

USE THIS SPACE TO CONTINUE EXPLORING!

WHAT DID YOU DISCOVER HERE?

At the top of the book on page XI, we asked you to reflect on what brought you to this book and what you hoped to glean from it. Go back now and read what you wrote. Did we deliver? Did you gain what you wanted? Or did you discover something unexpected? Explore how this book ultimately made you feel and what you discovered about yourself. Reflect away!

_____
_____
_____
_____
_____
_____
_____
_____
_____
_____
_____
_____
_____
_____
_____
_____
_____
_____
_____

REMINDER!

Don't forget to share your work with us! Remember all those brilliant insights, sketches, and explorations you had along the way? Snap a pic and shoot it our way! Share your writings! Upload your drawings! Show us your ofrendas and vision boards! Send anything and everything our way to submit@soulboom.com. We can't wait to see it.

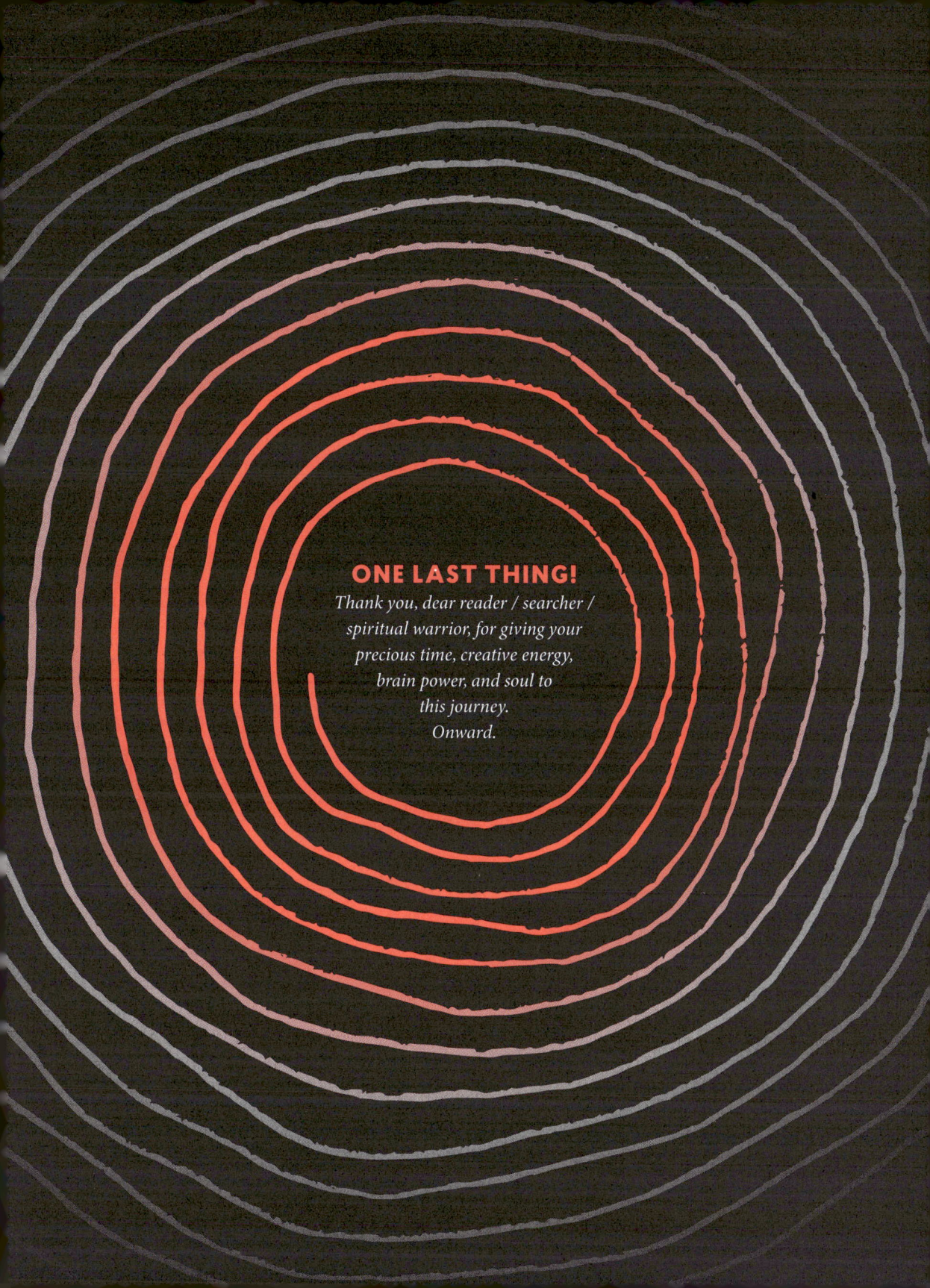

ONE LAST THING!
Thank you, dear reader / searcher / spiritual warrior, for giving your precious time, creative energy, brain power, and soul to this journey.
Onward.

Closing Thoughts

FOR ALL
WHO
SEARCH

WHEN we began writing the *Soul Boom Workbook*, we were convinced that the hardest unit of work to write would be Part Three, digging into the dark stuff of life—anxiety, suffering, and death. Turns out, we were wrong. The toughest unit was the final one, where we tried to explore how to build a better world.

We discovered that, at least for the two of us, it was easier to outline all the ways we can work on ourselves. Probably because it's work we've both undertaken! We know what it looks like to reflect, to grapple, to question, to search. So much of this book is about connecting with our inner selves—to bring to life the words of artist and poet Nayyirah Waheed, who wrote:

"And I said to my body, softly, 'I want to be your friend.'

"It took a long breath and replied, 'I have been waiting my whole life for this.'"

Only we wanted to befriend not our bodies but our souls—that was the idea we wanted these pages to deeply and wholly explore.

But figuring out how to intentionally—and in a spiritually grounded way—challenge and reinvent big, complicated systems to change the world? *Ridonkulous*.

As we began trying to craft the ideas and activities that would make building a better world both manageable and transformative, we realized we could have written an entire book about this one subject! (*Idea!* Pitch publisher a *Soul Boom for a Better World* book as the next one in this series.)

We repeatedly focused on the simplest ideas. How to intentionally gather. How to notice needs. What it means to lead with compassion. Why thinking locally matters. How to build capacity for change. And we think we did a pretty good job of introducing this giant, meaty, malleable field of work known as spiritually grounded social action.

That being said, through it all, we kept coming back to one thing: PEOPLE.

Yup. The weird, wonderful, diverse, strange, beautiful, and bizarre human beings with whom we share this planet just might be the key to a world-embracing spiritual revolution. Because no one changes the world—or even themselves—alone.

At a fundamental level, we are naturally drawn to do this work with the people who matter most to us. The folks we spend the most time with—our parents, spouses, siblings, children, best friends. We believe these ideas and conversations are vital to instill in our nuclear orbits. Doing that effectively, in order to empower a deeply spiritual and socially minded family, is a beast of a job and could *also* fill an entire book. (*Idea #2!* Pitch publisher a *Soul Boom for Families* book, too.)

However, venturing beyond our inner circles—that is hella hard. Our modern world sends us all sorts of mixed-up, messed-up ideas about other people. No one is to be trusted. People are cruel. Half the country are lunatics who want to destroy the nation. Everyone is out for themselves. We stay tightly knitted to the people closest to us because it's impossible to know the true intentions of another human being.

But maybe we've got it all backward. By emanating distrust toward our fellow humans, we are creating discord and disunity. Every faith tradition tells us that, instead, the solution is to radiate love toward others—unabashed, unhindered, freely sown LOVE.

Judaism teaches the importance of loving all creation. Christianity teaches us to love our neighbors as ourselves. Muslims are told to extend love to people of all faiths. And in our religion, the Baha'i Faith, we are taught that love should be extended to people of all races, religions, genders, and creeds, regardless of their background. The wise Baha'i spiritual leader 'Abdu'l-Baha describes it so: "Do not be content with showing friendship in words alone, let your heart burn with loving-kindness for all who may cross your path."

Even the Beatles proclaimed, "All you need is love." And we agree. Love is the greatest power in existence. Can you imagine if we all were walking around Earth wearing giant, hot-pink love filters over our eyes and hearts? So that any time we looked at another human or animal or natural wonder, we would just feel deep, powerful, overwhelming love for them? That our hearts would *burn* with loving-kindness? What a different (and likely more peaceful) world we would live in.

So as we leave you to continue your search for meaning, spirituality, joy, and community in your personal life, we want to encourage you to do this work as it was always meant to be done . . . with others, in a spirit of abounding love.

Explore what a spiritual revolution could look like with friends, neighbors, even strangers. And make it *FUN*. The work of the soul doesn't always have to be heavy or serious or reverent or woo-woo. It can be joyful and light. It can lift us up. Inspire us. Make us laugh.

So play Pictionary or Charades, *Soul Boom*-style. Gather your friends, write "high-level" spiritual concepts down (e.g., the soul, prayer, God, compassion), and put them in a bowl. Draw or act out the terms. Be playful.

Plan a "Stand Up, Sit Down" activity. Write a list of 30 statements ranging from silly ("I like ice cream more than popcorn.") to spiritual ("I believe in life after death."). Pick a statement at random and ask people to stand if they agree or stay seated if they don't. Let natural debate and consultation ensue.

Start a "moving spiritual stories" book club open to anyone! Read *Tao Te Ching* by Lao-tzu or *The Power of Now* by Eckhart Tolle or *Tiny Beautiful Things* by Cheryl Strayed or *Man's Search for Meaning* by Viktor Frankl. (In fact, shoot us an email at bookclub@soulboom.com, and we'll send you a whole reading list for a spiritually inspired book club!)

Organize a faith field trip for your community. Invite people to tour and visit your local houses of worship. A mosque. A synagogue. A Hindu temple. Share with each other the things that make you feel wonderful—or weird—about the experience. Better yet, take a class to learn more about the Bible or Quran, or join a Baha'i study circle to engage in a spiritual learning process about social action.

Plan a citywide volunteer day in conjunction with your city council to clean up the dilapidated yards of your elderly neighbors. Or an overrun park. Or a littered beach. Or just gather some friends and tools and help one neighbor mow their lawn and weed a flower patch.

Choose to become the *protagonist* of your spiritual transformation and journey. You are the *LEAD*. You don't need a priest or a giant temple or Burning Man. You and your community can do more than you think. So just do it.

And if all else fails, pick up a clean copy of the *Soul Boom Workbook* and do it with someone else . . . or several other people.

Our one human family, on this one planet we all share, is our superpower. As we know from Harvard University's Grant Study, our well-being is not determined by our successes or our wealth or even our health. The single, hands-down, greatest predictor of our happiness over the course of our lives is the quality of our relationships.

It's the people. So *Soul Boom*-lets, let's get to work. The spiritual revolution awaits. And you are the ones who will take us there.

—Rainn and Shabnam

ACKNOWLEDGMENTS

We have a lot of people to thank, and we are going to try to get through them as quickly as possible before the orchestra plays us off stage. Give us a few more minutes of your precious time and join us in thanking them.

First, we want to honor all the creative souls who took time to read our very first full draft of the manuscript and send us such thoughtful, challenging, and encouraging feedback. Jordan Raj, Golriz Lucina, Shawya Mogharabi, Samah Tokmachi—you are all amazing . . . go write your own books, so the world can appreciate your brilliance!

Steve Sarowitz, your passion is contagious. Big thanks to you, Ford Bowers, and EVERYONE at Companion Arts for being such devoted friends and vision-keepers. Y'all cook with fire.

Sara Critchfeld at Fetzer Institute—you're an OG inspiration expert, and you have connected so many dots for The Soul Boom Project. Bless you and the Fetzer team, each and every one.

Ken Bowers, it always makes us smile to hear your thoughts on our somewhat sacrilegious tomes.

Tiffany Stelmar, your behind-the-scenes support and research kept us from having to sift through Tim Tebow and Tony Robbins quotes in order to find the right insightful words to share. You took one for the team, and we thank you.

Speaking of which, thanks to all the brilliant folks (alive and dead) whose inspiring quotes we compiled in the margins that made us look hella smarter and wiser.

Charlotte Gordon Cumming, thank you for granting us permission to use your husband's words in our book. We hear the echoes of his footsteps in them.

Brian Chojnowski, who knew two simple colors could create beautiful art? Thanks for your amazing collaboration through this process and for your keen and magical eye!

Brant Rumble, who is just the most fantastic editor ever. Thanks for rolling the dice on this *Soul Boom* thing. Grand Central/Hachette, you're all right. (Though we still think you should adopt Google Docs into your workflow.)

And finally, thank you to all our Baha'i brothers and sisters for always having our backs along the way.

Shabnam also wants to thank:

My husband, Toufan Rahimpour. You're a good one. A kind heart. Thank you for doing all the diapers and swim classes and Costco runs this past year so I could make this weird and wonderful book. I love you mucho.

Ryder and Everest, you are hands-down the two greatest things I have ever contributed to this crazy planet. My heart explodes with love for you. To the ends of the universe and [*insert banjo sounds*] back.

Mom and Dad, your generosity knows no bounds. I hope to be just like you when I grow up. Nahal, Neilou, Shawya—you are and always will be my village. My ride-or-dies.

Last, to Rainn, thank you for being my co-conspirator for all these years. You challenge me. You are one of my best friends. And I love making cool, creative things with you. Let's do it again!

Rainn also wants to thank:

I want to thank my wife, Holiday, for her infinite levels of support, encouragement, and wisdom. I wouldn't be an artist without you and the boom of your beautiful soul.

Walter, my brilliant son, who is on his own spiritual journey, whether he knows it or not.

A thousand thank yous to Richard Abate, my book agent, who believed in this crazy *Soul Boom* endeavor before I did.

Big-hearted Kartik Chainani, who has produced the *Soul Boom* podcast and tended the *Soul Boom* brand and its social media garden like nobody's business.

Derik Smith rocks. As does Aaron Lee. But my uncle, Rhett Diessner, rocks hardest.

Also, Arthur Brooks is way kinder than he has any right to be.

My mom and stepdad, Shay and Chuck Cooper, I am so moved by your support, love, and your incredible *Soul Boom* hippie gatherings by the brook!

Shabnam, we've been through so much together, and I'm jumping with gratitude that we're working together again. You are literally the most capable, insightful, and joyful collaborator I've ever had the chance to work with. Onward to all our various *Soul*-named ventures!